The Breakdown of Europe

The Breakdown of Europe

Richard Body

New European Publications
London

Published in the United Kingdom in 1998 by
New European Publications Limited
14–16 Carroun Road
London SW8 1JT, England

Cover design Lloyd Allen
Typesetting Margaret Allen
Editing & Proof-reading Dr Lee Rotherham

British Library Cataloguing in Publication Data

ISBN 1-8724-1011-1

Printed and bound in Great Britain by Biddles Limited, Guildford, Surrey

Acknowledgments

Shortly before he died Leopold Kohr prompted me to write this book. No one by birth, upbringing, education and profession could be more truly European than he was, but to him the European Union was anathema. The true wealth of Europe was the glory of its immense diversity of cultures. In his view that diversity would be lost inexorably in any economic or political union – a "sludgy amalgam". Many of the arguments in this book, together with its title, spring from his masterpiece *The Breakdown of Nations*.

Margaret Clarke and Margaret Allen both laboured away at typing and typesetting as well as the infuriating task of doing so much of it again when I changed my mind. Maurice Temple Smith, who was emboldened enough to publish my first two books, gallantly edited the manuscript. Joy Michaud and Lee Rotherham have also given valuable help. To them I am more than grateful.

"To the size of states there is a limit as there is to plants, to animals and to implements; for none of these retain their power or facility when they are too large."

ARISTOTLE

Contents

Introduction   1

1. Power is Lovely (for some)   7

2. The Myth of the Big Market   15

3. War and Peace   25

4. The Disease of Growth   31

5. Bring on the Artist   45

6. Europe out of Control   51

7. Another Europe for the Electronic Age   63

8. As if People Mattered   71

    References   93

    Index   95

Introduction

There was a time when history seemed to offer such a simple lesson. Underlying all the turmoil of human affairs one steady movement could be discerned, an inexorable tendency for mankind to form itself into ever larger social and political units. Our most remote ancestors lived in family groups but the time came when, to satisfy some of their needs, they linked up with other groups to form tribes. As the centuries went by, tribes merged to become nations and these nations in turn, often under the stress of war, united into bigger nations, empires and unions of various kinds. This process is still at work and it will go on until eventually even the largest union, of a billion people or more, will not be large enough and a world government will take power.

It was, so we were told, futile to resist this great tide of history. Only sentimentalists and unthinking patriots would try to hold it back, and they would be not only ineffective but morally wrong. Nation states had from their beginning been embroiled in wars and the only way to free mankind from the horrors of conflict was to abolish the nation state. The syllogism was simple: the nation states cause wars; wars are bad; therefore nation states are bad.

This interpretation of history has persuaded many people that federalism is an inevitable and desirable step forward, and in this context federalism means the giving up of power and identity by each nation so that eventually the real political and social unit will be the federation itself. Among those who think like this are some sincere advocates of the European Union. They claim that for half a century it has saved Europe from war and that it will give her people a united strength to resist the encroachments of the world's super-powers – America today, China tomorrow – and the strength, too, not to be bullied by the huge multinational companies that are coming to dominate the world's economy.

This description of events is superficially persuasive. It is very convenient for those who stand to gain by the process it describes. And, like all seductively simple theories of history, it is wrong.

First, this one-way movement is not what is happening in the world today. The number of nation states, so far from diminishing, is increasing. If that seems surprising, the figures are given in Chapter 1.

Second, it is not the nation state that is now the cause of war. Although the years since 1945 have seen a continuous succession of wars throughout the world, surprisingly few of them have been between nation states. The great majority have been, in effect, civil wars. They have occurred in states within which unwilling populations were yoked together in unions that they resented and that had often been imposed on them by outside powers. Yugoslavia, Nigeria, Chechnya have been typical examples of late-twentieth-century conflict. The Franco-German wars belonged to an earlier epoch.

Third, it is not true that countries that have refused to pool their sovereignty have proved helpless in the face of global economic forces. Within Europe, for example, Switzerland and Norway have irritatingly refused to go down the drain of history and are, in fact, thriving mightily. Chapter 2 provides some figures that show the actual economic results of joining or not joining the European Union.

Switzerland is perhaps the supreme proof that, in order to trade widely and profitably throughout the world, it is not necessary to be part of a large political entity. It is important to distinguish between political boundaries and market limits and this is where the question of free trade versus protectionism comes in. This is one of those issues that are greatly complicated by modern technical and commercial developments. On the one hand, there is the right of a willing vendor and a willing purchaser to enter an agreement whereby one sells what the other wants only at a price that both consider fair. That the two persons live in different countries ought to be irrelevant. On the other hand, there is the uncomfortable fact that the wage cost of producing a car (including social security contributions) are twenty times higher in Coventry than in China. Do we dare abandon all protection? And does membership of the European Union help or hinder us?

In the real world the effects of any big movement such as the emergence of the global market are always complex and often paradoxical. Some of them are explored in Chapter 7, including the radical changes brought about by information technology. There is also the interesting counter-current described by John Naisbitt in his book *Global Paradox*, in which he argues that, as economies merge, there is a reaction in which people with a linguistic or cultural identity strive for political independence.

Finally and most importantly, we have to consider the social, cultural and human effects of living in a very big political unit. This is the major theme of this book. Here the results of any unbiased enquiry are inescapable. For a start, the level of crime and alienation is an index of the basic health or ill-health of a society, and it is consistently higher in big states than in small. To see why, we need only to ask whether it is the small country or the super-state that best allows its citizens to identify with it and to feel that sense of belonging that leads to a willing acceptance of social responsibilities. If that sense is missing, will any amount of policing or prison-building give us a law-abiding, stable and happy society?

The sense of alienation is felt not only by poor people in deprived inner-city areas. Disillusionment with the process of how they are governed is gaining ground among millions of people across Western Europe. It is evident, too, in the United States and indeed in nearly all parts of the developed world. It would seem that only in the smaller democracies, notably Norway, Switzerland and New Zealand, is there little or no disillusionment.

There is a further uncomfortable fact for the lovers of size. The mega-state does not deliver on its financial promises. So far from being an efficient economical form of organisation, it is in fact an expensive and cumbersome one: the costs of all forms of administration are higher in big states. Every organisation has a certain optimum size for fulfilling its objectives, and it is just as uneconomical to go above that size as to fall below it. The extravagance of the European Union's bureaucracy is notorious – indeed scandalous – but even if it were far more tightly controlled it would still be unnecessarily costly. The way it is designed fails to take account of the fact that different functions need organisations of different sizes to carry them out, and the attempt to have so many disparate functions all performed by a Europe-wide bureaucracy is bound to be ludicrously inefficient.

There is a universal truth about all the states in the developed world. Once they exceed a certain size, the welfare of their people – materially, socially and politically – diminishes. Both the people and the state become diseased. The symptoms of this disease are evident in every mega-state, in crime, social division, and bloated bureaucracy, and in the mind of a great majority, a sense of powerlessness.

Unfortunately the tendency to centralise power in Europe is continuing as strongly as ever. The introduction of a single currency would be a big further step in that direction and there is no sign that those who are making the running have seen the dangers ahead. First, they do not understand what deep changes to the structure of the European Union will have to be made if it is to become a truly European organisation. At present only a minority of European states belong to it, containing a minority of Europe's population. This state of affairs is not going to last for ever, and the pressures to enlarge the union are growing stronger. The states of eastern Europe are on the doorstep and they will not be content to have escaped the domination of Moscow only to replace it with the domination of Brussels.

The ultimate danger facing the European Union is that of disintegration. The new states that have emerged in the world in recent decades have mostly done so by breaking away from larger federations or empires. Their peoples were no longer willing to be governed by those they regarded as foreigners even if technically they were citizens of the same union. It is much more likely than it is generally realised that the peoples of Europe will grow increasingly restless when they find that their ability to govern themselves has been taken away from them. Ordinary people have always been far less convinced than their rulers about the benefits of a political union of Europe, as they have showed on the few occasions when they have been consulted in referendums. The margins in favour have been modest, despite the millions of pounds spent on propaganda from the European Union's own funds and from those of the giant companies that hope to benefit. As the social and economic disadvantages of over-centralisation become unmistakably clear it will be very surprising if the world-wide demand for independence by small nations does not spread to Europe. When it does, much of the elaborate and expensive apparatus of political union will have to be dismantled.

Those who favour a federal union of Europe like to present their opponents as jingoists who would drag us all back into a confusion of antagonistic states that resented having to co-operate over anything. This, it need hardly be said, is nonsense. What we need is a different type of co-operation, a loose association of nation states to agree common policy in certain specific areas. No one denies that there are things that must be done internationally if they are to be done at all. The environment provides an obvious example. It is no good one country trying to keep its

4

rivers clean if the country upstream is pouring in toxic effluents. It is no good having a clean air policy if your forests are dying from acid rain produced by your neighbour's chimneys. Such problems demand inter-governmental action. Other problems need world-wide co-operation.

In *Europe of Many Circles* I set out in some detail how this can be achieved. Increasingly, though, inter-governmental co-operation on a continental scale will not be enough. Already we have a catalogue of problems in need of global solutions: global warming, the continual destruction of the rain forests, and the rapid depletion of marine life by industrial fishing are obvious candidates for co-operative action on a world-wide scale.

No common policy, whether continental or global, is likely to be enforceable unless laws are made or revenue raised. The question is, should either of these two powers of coercion be exercised inter-governmentally or supra-governmentally? The latter is the path chosen by the European Union; and this book argues it is inherently undemocratic and will lead to friction and disharmony when the legitimate interests of minorities come to be overridden. It is also unnecessary. The inter-governmental approach is the alternative adopted by countries that believe it is in their interests to co-operate with others to overcome a common problem, thus achieving with others what they cannot achieve by themselves. Sovereignty then is not surrendered.

In the European debate, no word, not even democracy, has been more misused than sovereignty. As international lawyers recognise, sovereignty is a hallmark or the touchstone of the nation state. A people or nation are formed into a nation state when they possess the five elements of sovereignty: the sovereign (i.e. supreme and exclusive) power to make all their own laws, the sovereign power to interpret them in their own courts, the sovereign power over all taxation, the sovereign power to enter into all treaties with other states, and the sovereign power to declare war. Only the last of those remains exclusively in the hands of the individual member-states of the European Union. Each of the others have been eroded to a greater or lesser extent.

The inter-governmental approach does nothing to take away the sovereign powers of the people: their nation state endures. This book contends there is nothing undesirable about the nation state, provided it co-operates with others (as it must out of sheer self-interest) and does not become too big. Excessive bigness is easily defined. A nation state is too big if its sheer size entitles it to overwhelm its neighbours economically, militarily, or diplomatically; and within itself the nation state is too big if its people feel themselves powerless in respect of the sovereign powers exercised over them.

To merge different peoples together in some kind of federal union or under a supranational government can succeed as Chapter 8 shows, but those conditions do not and cannot exist in Europe. The Continent is too rich in diversity for the attempt to succeed. That diversity is its true wealth and its glory – only the truly European seems to understand that and it is now at risk.

At base, the European issue is a battle about power. Two small groups of people have a thirst for the power that resides at the heart of the European Union. The heads of the great business corporations with operations across many national frontiers do not wish to be hindered by the regulations of those numerous different countries, especially when their governments try to protect the interests of their own people; far better to deal with just the Eurocrats of Brussels in a single market with harmonised regulations. The other group consists of government ministers. It may seem a paradox for them to surrender the self-government of their nation, but what is surrendered is the power of both Parliament and the media to control them. If policies can be agreed, laws made, and revenue raised by them and their counterparts from other member-states, alone and in secret, in the absence of interfering parliamentarians or questioning journalists, it is exceedingly agreeable.

In the process, all others outside those two small groups become demeaned and belittled. It is time to remember J. S. Mill's wise words: "The state should never pursue even great ends by means which make its citizens small." It is also time to consider why the mega-state is so attractive to those intoxicated by power.

1

Power is Lovely (for some)

Politics is about getting and using power. It was Lenin, no mean practitioner of the art, who put the central question most tersely: "Who, whom?" – who has power over whom? Even if we reject the idea that political units must inevitably go on getting bigger it is clear that there are very strong forces thrusting in that direction, and not the least of them is the love of power.

In his book *The Breakdown of Nations*, Leopold Kohr introduced his readers to a new subject, social morphology, the study of how society becomes diseased by the cancer of excessive growth. Every society, he argues, has an optimum size, and if it is larger or smaller than that size it will be less efficient. If it is too small it can be brought up to the optimum by an increase in population, but if it is too large it can be cured only by major surgery, by dividing itself up into smaller units. In reality not many nations are too small, and the people of Liechtenstein, for one, would deny that having a population of only 26,000 is a handicap to congenial living.

To Kohr, the excessive size of a state is the fundamental cause of human misery. Other causes obviously exist, such as greed, cruelty and selfishness, but their scope is less in a small state and can even be altogether absent. As states grow larger, human beings find it easier to be nastier and get away with it. The freedom of the individual, the principles of justice, democracy itself, all are weakened as the state grows larger.

Kohr did not explain why states, corporations, and other units of society outgrow their optimum size, but certainly the love of power must be a major cause. Politicians and civil servants do not declare to the world that their ambition is to gain power over other people: what motivates them – naturally – is an idealistic wish to better the world. Perhaps only a cynic would deny that this wish does genuinely exist in many of them, and it would be absurd to consider all heads of large states or major corporations as megalomaniacs, but it is naive to underrate the attractions of power. It is, as Henry Kissinger is said to have remarked, the greatest aphrodisiac, and just as no general wants to command a smaller army, few politicians willingly restrict the area of their own power. Usually they have had to pay quite a heavy price in their own lives to achieve it. Francis Bacon, who dedicated his life to self-advancement, described the task as climbing up a winding stair. It demands planning, determination, usually some deviousness, but above all a thirst for power.

Politics, even democratic politics, must unavoidably be carried on in an environment where pursuit of power is the normal and accepted thing. It must be so, for without power nothing could be done to better a state or even to prevent it declining into anarchy. But in such an atmosphere it is very important that the dangers should be recognised and limits set up.

The appetite for power grows with feeding and history is full of examples of rulers who have started out with good intentions, even with high achievements, and ended as brutal despots. One of the best examples is Ivan the Terrible. He became Tsar of Russia in 1547 and for six years pursued a programme of liberal reform. He devolved the power of central government to local communities, remodeled the army, reformed the legal code, and established the rudiments of a parliament, which he and his ministers consulted. Then power turned his head. He reversed the reforms and Russia sank into a hideous tyranny. Among the changes he made was the division of his country into two. One half was to revert to feudal rule, while the other, known as the *Oprichnina*, was to be under his absolute control. Two thousand thugs were put into black uniforms, given the name *Oprichniki*, and let loose upon his subjects, licensed to enforce his decrees as they thought fit.

Lord Acton's famous dictum about absolute power is often misquoted and it is relevant to our argument to set it in its context. I have in front of me a facsimile of a letter Acton wrote on 5 April 1857 to Mantell Creighton, Bishop of London. In his *History of the Papacy,* Creighton had failed, in Acton's view, to pass proper judgement on the secular power of the Renaissance popes and the use they made of it. "I cannot accept," Lord Acton wrote, "your canon that we are to judge pope and king unlike other men, with a favourable presumption that they did no wrong. If there is any presumption, it is the other way against the holders of power. Historic responsibility has to make up for that want of legal responsibility. Power tends to corrupt, and absolute power corrupts absolutely. Great men are almost always bad men, even when they exercise influence and not authority."

In my own experience it is certainly true that people with a strong desire for power are usually psychologically damaged. Over more than forty years of active political life I have seen several hundred colleagues enter Parliament. It has not been difficult to analyse various motives, and usually a blend of two or three. Those moved by the appetite for power are the hardest to detect, for it is usually concealed and often only shows when power is attained and enjoyed. Nonetheless there are signs to flash a warning. In his *Psychology of Military Incompetence,* Norman Dixon, Reader in Psychology at University College, London, was able to draw on his considerable experience as a soldier. He wrote of the kind of man who joins the army to gain authority over others, and their characteristics are very similar to those of the young politician with the same drive. It is also worth studying M. L. Farber's thesis 'The Anal Character and Political Aggression' in the *Journal of Abnormal Social Psychology*, 1955.

Often it is a sense of inferiority or rejection that propels the power-hungry. To understand their careers we should look less to political philosophy and more to their relationships with their parents, particularly their mothers. If they feel 'not good enough', or their mothers rejected them or made them feel inadequate, it can set off a psychopathic anxiety that determines the whole course of their lives. Such neuroses can be treated with drugs, usually in the benzodiazepine group, but their efficacy is lost after a while and they also bring about a lack of concentration in the patient, so little may be gained. In reality the drug such people most often have recourse to is alcohol. Middle-aged politicians who see their goals slipping away – and civil servants too – often seek the solace of the bottle. Without being unkind, the rest of us may feel a little relieved that someone who was climbing up the greasy pole for the wrong reasons is now slipping towards the bottom.

If the desire for power among our rulers tends to push us towards larger political units, it is also true that as units grow larger, so does the tendency for them to be governed by the power-hungry. The bigger the nation, the bigger will be the numbers of people competing to rule it and the more powerful the motivation they will need if they are to

9

succeed. The greasy pole is higher and the number of people jostling around it is larger. Not much ambition is required to become chairman of some local authority that has modest powers over a small population. One needs far less strength of character, and far less ruthlessness, to become Mayor of Toytown than to become the dictator of a superstate and to maintain oneself in that position while other aspirants eagerly try to pull one down. Many a small state is like Toytown: its head of state may strut around his little stage but his subjects will probably not be very frightened of him. Of course there have been despotic and even terrifying rulers of small states – think of Papa Doc in Haiti – but the point is that it is not necessary for their rulers to be in love with power. They can be people of a far more modest cast of mind and if all the superstates were presided over by the kind of people who become Mayors of Toytown the world would almost certainly be a safer place. As it is, the leaders of superstates are propelled to their seats of power by a driving force that can only be explained in psychological terms.

The present century has seen the arrival of another vehicle for the power-hungry: the transnational corporation. As trade barriers fall and communications improve they can be truly be called global corporations, for if they cannot yet operate in every corner of the globe, it is their ambition to do so. Although the men and women entering the business world mostly do so in pursuit of money rather than power, there can be no doubt that the heads of global corporations do exercise great powers, greater, it is often said, than that of any nation's president. Certainly these people do affect our lives a thousandfold more than the head of a modest business or county bank of generations ago. As great men are they, as Lord Acton would assert, almost inevitably bad men?

To counterbalance that power many people believe it is necessary to create ever larger political units. As we shall see, this belief is untrue, but it exemplifies the way in which bigness begets bigness. In the past it has been politics, and above all armed force, that has been the motive power in this. Large states can dominate and threaten their weaker neighbours, eventually swallowing them up or forcing them to coalesce into states that are big enough to resist aggression. To describe this process as 'progress' would be mistaken. The resulting large states are not more efficient nor can they command the loyalty of their citizens so well. They are the product of a pathological condition resulting from the lust for power.

Obviously it is easier for power to be misused in an autocracy than in a democracy. It is tempting to believe that autocracy is a thing of the past, but we should remember that in Europe's history autocracies have far

10

exceeded democracies in number and the most repressive dictatorships of all occurred in our own century. Even today, in the world as a whole, autocracy is the norm. In only a few of its 180-or-so independent states can one be reasonably certain that the governments will change without the use of force. It would be dangerously over-optimistic to plan our world on the assumption that democracy is, or soon will be, universal and lasting. Instead we should acknowledge that when tyranny does occur its ill-effects are in proportion to the size of the state it rules. Mao and Stalin were able to inflict misery that not only affected more people but also went deeper than anything Castro could have done in Cuba. The larger the state, the more remote its rulers are from the people they rule, and the weaker the restraints on them. Edmund Burke warned us that power can be intoxicating. The only way of cutting autocrats down to size is to cut down the size of the territory over which they exercise dominion.

This whole question of power is directly relevant to the decisions we face in Europe today. Again, a little background history can help. The unification of our Continent was first attempted under the Roman Empire and incidentally it was Caligula, one of the worst of the Roman emperors and one of the most deeply corrupted by the exercise of power, who so revelled in the rape of the German marches. Since then there have been various attempts at unification. Charlemagne went some way, Napoleon briefly went still further. Hitler nearly succeeded, and it is interesting that his New Economic Order was in essence very similar to the European Economic Community. Even Ivan the Terrible saw himself as European rather than Russian, immersing himself in European history and, in his earlier years, studying the Dutch and English systems of government with a view to making them paradigms for Russia. Once he even declared a wish to settle in England, where he said he would feel at home!

All those attempts at unification failed, but not before they had brought misery to millions and threatened the true wealth of Europe, which lies in its diversity and its remarkable attainments in all fields of art and culture. This is something that should be in the forefront of our minds now that we are confronted by an apparently inexorable process of globalisation – a horrid word to describe a horrid happening. Mass communication, mass transport, mass production and mass marketing are giving us a mass society, homogenised throughout the world. A piece of gadgetry hurtling above the globe enables a bush fire in Australia to be seen within a fraction of a second on screens in Johannesburg and Chicago. Travelling through Arab countries the easiest two words to learn to read in Arab script (because they are the ones most commonly displayed on public hoardings) are 'Coca' and 'Cola'. Walk into an expensive hotel in England or South East Asia and about the only difference you will find between them is that in the former the bar is decorated with artificial palm trees and is trying to look tropical while in the latter it is panelled in fake oak and called 'The London Pub'. At a time like this it is overwhelmingly important to preserve diversity: any centralising tendency that threatens it should be treated with the deepest suspicion.

We should also remember that globalisation concentrates in a few hands and take steps to curb not increase it. This is true throughout the world but particularly with Europe. If the European Union succeeds in evolving into a superstate the winding stair that leads to the top will be higher and command a greater domain than in any of the member states. The temptation to climb it will be even more irresistible, especially to those with a thirst for power, and when they get power they will exercise it to the limit. Power concentrated at the centre will be used to enhance its power still more, and as this process goes on there will be ever more integration, harmonisation, and uniformity. And those who are in charge will not be chosen from the saintly souls to whom we would confidently give authority over our lives, knowing that they would never wish to exercise power for power's sake. No doubt there are saintly people in the world. They would not filch the silver teaspoons when we left the room or molest our children after collecting them from school and if they were elected to some high office their kindly natures would endure. The trouble is that such people, lacking the drive for power, do not rise to the top of huge political structures, and if they ever do they would not stay there for long.

So must we despair, accepting that the forces making for centralisation and giantism are so overwhelming that they cannot be resisted? I think not. An interesting counter tendency is at work in the world, and it too has great strength. We noted John Naisbitt's argument in *Global Paradox* that as the economies of the world merge together there is a reaction in which peoples with linguistic or cultural identity strive for political independence. His book was given the *World Review* Award for the most important book on world affairs in 1996 and its thesis is clearly born out by the facts. Within the United Kingdom all four component countries (which include England) contain substantial numbers of people who would prefer to be independent of the other three members, and it is clear that some measure of devolution is on its way. In the world at large a similar desire has led to a great increase in the number of nation states. In 1946 the United Nations could recruit only 51 members: by the 1990's 186 had

12

qualified to join. Many of these are the erstwhile colonies, dependencies and protectorates of Western Europe, but about half of them have come into being after the process of decolonisation. Some of the new members are very small but have nevertheless proved themselves politically and economically viable. Andorra, with a population of 47,000, is a notable example. It has a seat in the United Nations, the right to an Olympic team, its own currency, and a separate international dialling code. It also has the intangible but inestimable benefit of its people's self-esteem as an independent nation.

The creation of another country is usually the result of a civil war, or at least some violent conflict between peoples living within the same nation state. It is conflicts of this kind that have accounted for most of the wars since 1945. Some major wars, such as Korea and Vietnam, were surrogate conflicts between super-powers, but the number of wars between ordinary nation states has been a tiny proportion of the whole.

People do not go through the horror of civil war unless they feel that they have a very strong motive. The history of the last fifty years should surely teach us that unwise unification and centralisation can generate powerful centrifugal forces. Like a lump of uranium that exceeds the critical mass, a state that has been enlarged and unified beyond the tolerance of its peoples is likely to fly apart in a most destructive way. Ordinary men and women are ready to pay the highest price to defend their communal identity. It is dangerous to override that impulse in an attempt to gain the supposed benefits of large-scale political units. In any case, as we shall now see, when those benefits are examined objectively, most of them turn out to be illusory.

2

The Myth of the Big Market

It has become an accepted fact that prosperity demands big markets. Division of labour, the economies of scale, the ability to fund research and development; all these depend on selling large quantities of the final product, and that depends on having a large enough market in which to sell it.

There is, of course, an important truth here. An Andorran car manufacturer whose market was confined to Andorra could never be in the forefront of automobile engineering. No small company selling in a small market could produce the Jumbo Jet or most of the new drugs that now cure diseases. Nevertheless, while keeping this truth in mind, it is important not to be led on into other assertions that do not really follow from it.

An initial problem arises in defining what we mean by prosperity. Economists measure it in terms of output and prices, but that can be misleading. For example, one couple may choose to furnish their house with cheap chairs that last a few years and then have to be thrown away. Another may buy one set of chairs that are still in use by their grandchildren, by then valuable antiques. The first couple will in the end spend more and so their furniture will have made a greater contribution to their country's gross domestic product; but is it really a sign of wealth to live with shoddy furniture rather than with something beautiful and durable and built by a craftsman who took pride in his work?

In such instances the chief effect of a large market is not to increase real prosperity but to allow the existence of mass-marketing, driven by mass-advertising, which can coax the public into spending its money in ways it would not rationally choose. Of course, there are people who can only afford the cheapest, and others who believe they can only afford the cheapest and do not appreciate that they would be better off if they postponed the purchase of something else. There are also those who are ruled by fashion and a large number who just like their possessions to look new. These people are helped by mass-marketing, but the rest of us ought to be alert to its dangers, to recognise how and why our wealth is increased, and the ways in which it is eroded.

It is surely eroded when advertising persuades us to buy some ephemeral and unnecessary object rather than spending the money on, say, adequate dental care; when it persuades someone who would have had a lifetime's pleasure from owning a library of the world's great classics to spend thousands of pounds on an unnecessarily expensive car instead. His choice is distorted by the fact that while second-hand bookshops cannot afford to advertise, the car-makers spend many millions pushing their wares.

Some of us will still prefer books and the dentistry: our set of values determines our choice. The advertising industry must in the end work to change people's sense of values because otherwise it can have only a limited effect. The fact that is has succeeded in doing so is demonstrated by the way it has grown in recent decades. The major agencies spend hundreds of millions of pounds every year and its leaders have made vast fortunes. They would not be able to do that if their clients did not find them effective in changing the public's pattern of consumption.

Overall, the chief change in values produced by advertising is in favour of heavy spending on mass-produced consumer goods. It is always easier to talk people into preferring 'more' to 'better'. This may not correspond with their real desires or well-being and the distortion is bound to be worse in big markets because they allow – and indeed force – manufacturers to spend a higher proportion of the retail price of their products on advertising.

Another way in which the erosion of real wealth can take place is by the destruction of small businesses that cannot afford expensive advertising. In an expanding economy large-scale industries can grow in size without causing a corresponding fall in the number of small businesses, but each period of growth is followed by a plateau of nil growth or, more likely, a

16

recession and then it is the small businesses that go under. For over a century that has been a fact of economic history.

What has also been clear from history is that the smaller the market the less serious is any period of recession. Major slumps are the product of large markets. A typical depressed town is to be found where two or three very large businesses have been the backbone of the local economy and, having established their dominant position in the area, have miscalculated their markets or found the demand for their products falling off.

The company capable of causing most damage is the one that has acquired a dominant position in a large market. Sloth sets in. Why innovate if the product still sells? Why worry too much about maintaining good industrial relations when a near-monopoly makes you impervious to the consequences of restrictive practices? Why fight against excessive wage demands when the cost can be passed on to a captive customer? The British shipbuilding industry once had such a dominant position in the largest market of all – the world – and in that lay the seeds of its own decay. Any large protected market, such as the European Union single market, contains this danger. It can give large companies the opportunity to grow very large indeed; then, once they have achieved a dominant place in the protected market, decline can set in, thousands of jobs can be in jeopardy, and whole areas might be blighted.

The town or industry in which work is distributed over a thousand firms, each with a small number of people on the payroll, is much less vulnerable to depression. Depressed areas crying out for regional aid are not a feature of the small state; in large integrated markets they seem to be endemic.

There are ways, then, in which the 'wealth' produced by big companies and big markets is illusory. Nevertheless, it is a truism that we live in the age of the global market and the question is how we respond to it. One argument produced by those who favour big states, and in particular a federal integrated Europe, is that only large, powerful political units can stand up to the 'economic imperialism' of the mega-states that already exist, such as the USA, or the still more formidable ones that are coming into existence, such as China.

The trouble with this argument is that it refers to a world of the past. In earlier times individual states tried to protect their own agriculture and industries by imposing tariff barriers against imports, and it was often true that a political border could also be the boundary of a market. Today there is less of that protectionism and, economically, political borders have become less important. This, after all, is what the global economy is about. Provided a manufacturer is free to sell his products in a large enough market, he does not need the countries in that market to be politically united. There are, as we shall see, reasons why he may prefer them to be so, but those reasons do not always work to the benefit of the peoples concerned.

In standing up to the economic power of the mega-states the important thing is simply economic efficiency. The USA has certainly used political pressure to further the interests of its industrialists, but in the end it is the market that decides. General Motors cannot hope to go on selling its cars in Europe if European manufacturers can produce cars that are better or cheaper or more suited to local conditions. Efficiency of that kind does depend on access to a sufficient market and it is helped by having a home market within a large free-trade area; but the existence of an over-arching political authority to control that area is another matter. There is now a consensus across the political parties that government interference in industry and commerce, however well-meaning, is likely to do more harm than good if it goes beyond quite modest aims. This is increasingly recognised with individual states: it is even more true of supranational governments.

The real and present danger to our welfare lies not in the superstates but in the rise of the Eastern economies, where the greatest boom in the world history is taking place. In 1997 the economy of China grew at the rate of 12 per cent, in Singapore at 11 per cent, in Malaysia at 8 per cent, in Indonesia at 6 per cent and even in India, the laggard of Asia, at 4.5 per cent. This portends an explosion of purchasing power for many hundreds of millions of people; it will also put an intense and unsustainable demand on the world's resources. 1998 has seen a set-back, which in the long-term will be no more than a bad hiccup.

Europe and the USA will before long find themselves at a critical point. It may not matter very much that they fail to grow rapidly: the real threat is the actual decline of capital and jobs being sucked away from them, leading to a massive transfer of wealth from the West to the East. The boom is unstoppable; the wonder of electronic gadgetry will see to that. As ever more industrial production yields to this new technology, so the new plants, factories, and home-based industries will rise up in Asia. Whatever is now manufactured in Birmingham, Lyons, Frankfurt, Milan, or Pittsburgh will be made far more cheaply in one of the emerging economies of the East, where people are willing to work long hours for low wages with negligible regulations about health, safety, and hygiene. Wage costs may be one tenth or less of what they are in the European

18

Union or the USA: Sir James Goldsmith reckoned that a Frenchman's wages were 47 times those of a Vietnamese. Furthermore, half the Frenchman's wages go to the government, and the two most formidable items of government expenditure in the West are on the social services and the national debt, neither of which features significantly in the emerging economies. If unemployment rises, everyone in employment will have to pay more in taxes, but that will reduce their purchasing power which will mean more jobs lost and less encouragement to work. The flight of wealth from West to East will be accelerated.

All this, it can be said, is only fair. The people of the West have enjoyed a high standard of living, arguably to some extent at the expense of the Asians. In a just world the time has come for an equitable redistribution of the world's wealth; but when the Frenchman and the Vietnamese come to have an equal share, a fearful change will be forced on France.

It is not only jobs that will be drawn away to the East. The average rate of return on capital investment in the Asian countries is 20 per cent, so they will have no difficulty in attracting the money to capitalise their new industries and to enable one or two billion people to spend twice as much as they do now. This will impose enormous strains on the monetary policies of Western nations. To keep capital at home, in the face of such lucrative opportunities in the East, could mean forcing interest rates up to a penal level capable of frustrating large-scale investment and with a shattering effect on the West's economy.

Once again, political authority is not relevant to this problem. Governments, in the post-1945 decades, tried to restrict movements of capital by imposing exchange controls. The sale of a nation's currency in foreign markets was prohibited except under licence, which would only be given to pay for essential imports. Not even the most *dirigiste* government resorts to such a measure today. Exchange controls are now the mark of a totalitarian state, and even if attempts were made to apply them they would be ineffective. There are plenty of offshore devices for moving capital around the world, while banks, pension funds and other financial institutions have become so transnational in their operations that no state, however large, can override their powers of investment.

Nevertheless, even if government power to resist these pressures is limited, they make it doubtful whether the ideal of free trade throughout the world can now be achieved. Free trade had very strong arguments to support it. It allows goods to be produced in the most efficient place; it gives everyone the greatest choice of what to buy and where to obtain it;

19

it allows poor countries to compete freely and so raise their standards of living. It also reduces the chance of wars, since nations do not willingly go to war with their trading partners. As the old Victorian free traders used to say, when goods cannot cross frontiers the armies will. But for all these advantages it is hard to maintain an open, unprotected market when one is faced with rival producers willing to work for a tiny fraction of what one regards as a living wage.

The problem is just as acute when a country is faced with the 'dumping' of some product produced elsewhere. Manufacturers sometimes find it worthwhile to sell part of their output below the full cost of production and by doing so they can force an entry into a new market where the indigenous producers cannot compete against such artificially cheap prices. The local industry can be strangled and the outsider can then take over the market.

One of the advantages claimed for a federal Europe is that it will be big enough and strong enough to protect its members against this sort of thing. Once again, though, this strength turns out to be largely illusory. The problem lies in the diversity of the nations within the federation, for each will have different industries that need protection. A flood of cheap coal, for example, will be a serious threat to a country where mining is an important part of the economy, but a useful source of cheap energy for others that have no coal of their own. A tariff set for the federation as a whole is bound to be damaging to one of these interests, and we know from experience that what will actually happen will be a bout of political horse-trading, at the end of which the disgruntled country will have been placated with some concessions and favours, but nobody fully satisfied.

It is here that we come up against the vital distinction between a customs union and a free trade area. The latter is just what is says – an area within which states can trade freely with each other, unhindered by tariffs or other restraints. In trading with outside countries each state is free to set its own rules. That freedom is taken away from it in a customs union. Only the union, acting supranationally and on behalf of all its member states, has the power to take action. From its outset the European Union has been designed as a customs union and British industry has experience of what happens when one country is being injured by blatant acts of dumping while other member-states simply enjoy being able to buy the goods at knock-down prices.

At best the European Union's reaction to dumping is bound to be slow, with fifteen member-states needing to reach agreement. Decisions are complicated, too, by the fact that dumping can take an almost infinite number of possible forms so that its definition is open to debate. It is much easier for a single state to decide when it is threatened by dumping and to take appropriate action. There are limits on what it can do, imposed by the World Trade Organisation (successor to GATT), but not much ingenuity is needed to devise a non-tariff barrier. Small countries such as Switzerland, Iceland and even Liechtenstein have imposed such barriers against outside competition and have done so with impunity. Indeed it could be said that this is one of the reasons for their prosperity, for in a small country even the most minor industries are noticed and their plight is known to those responsible for trade policy.

There is a further argument which is often produced to show that in the world today the nation state is obsolete and must be replaced by larger unions. This is its impotence in the face of the huge and growing power of the great transnational corporations. The ten largest of these corporations have sales that exceed the gross domestic product of over eighty nation states and several of them have revenues as large as those of a medium-sized country. It is often said that if General Motors were a state it would have the world's twentieth largest economy, and it is not the largest of the multinationals.

In theory a nation state has the power to overrule any corporation, even a multinational. In reality that power can be hard to exercise. Once a corporation has settled part of its operations in a country, a considerable expense, it will be unwilling to uproot itself and may make some concessions. But interference beyond a certain point will bring the threat of withdrawal, and the politician is soon scared off by the fear of lost revenue, lost exports, and lost jobs. The governments of the host countries have come to see the hazards of interventionism and a *modus vivendi* has been worked out in most of the areas where the multinationals operate. This is even coming to be true in Eastern Europe.

Insofar as the interests of a transnational corporation may not always coincide with the interests of the host country, what political structure offers the best chance of protecting that country? Is it the nation state or some supranational organisation? Specifically, could the European Union control one of these great corporations better than Britain or France or Germany could do separately?

Initially it is tempting to say "yes": the threat of being excluded from union of fifteen states is clearly more powerful than the threat of being excluded from any one of them. Once again, though, a gap opens up between theory and practice. A number of small states can provide a kind of defence in depth; if a single central authority negotiates for them all it is only necessary to influence or browbeat that authority and the game is won. It is significant that the great multinationals have always been enthusiasts for the European Union and have contributed large sums of money to the various political bodies that have campaigned for closer European integration. The single market has been their objective, and the larger it is the better. To them, a multiplicity of small states with a variety of laws and taxes is an irritant; what they want is uniformity throughout a large market. This is clearly in their interests, but unfortunately, as economists agree, it is disadvantageous to companies of medium size and a matter of indifference to the very small.

Visitors to Brussels who look up the yellow page telephone directory will find in it the names of all the famous global corporations, European or otherwise. Not all of them are trading or manufacturing in Belgium but they all have offices close to the European Union headquarters. It is their listening post and the base from which they lobby. It is not difficult for their representatives to meet the officials who draft the directives regulating their industries. The Commission's staff have open doors; they are there in their offices, ready to be consulted or persuaded, and like those high up in any large, powerful and well-paid organisation, they have a natural sympathy with others of the same kind. Even if a small businessman could afford that kind of lobbying he would find himself dealing with people who had little understanding of his world and less sympathy.

The European Union has immense powers to regulate the internal market and to negotiate external trade policy, and one can be certain that they will be used to protect the interests of the big corporations, including the transnationals. It is true in general that centralisation of power and uniformity of conditions unquestionably favour the largest companies and disfavour their smaller rivals. This is dangerous in two ways. First, it obviously damages the small business by disproportionately favouring its large rivals, and it is small businesses that contribute most to the growth of employment and to flexibility in responding to changing opportunities. It is no coincidence that as continental Europe has more and more acceded to the demands of the biggest companies the problem of unemployment has become acute.

The second threat is that in this case the lion takes over the role of the tamer. Instead of the federation of European states becoming strong enough to resist the transnational corporations it has become their instrument. The hugely expensive campaign those corporations mounted to bring public opinion round in favour of 'Europe' (not least through cajoling the opinion-formers in the different parts of the media) has had its effect. We now face a real danger that the member states will be so changed by the Treaties of Rome and Maastricht that they will no longer be nation-states. So far from combining successfully to defend themselves against the over-mighty transnationals they will have devised the mechanism by which the transnationals were able to play a large part in bringing the nation state to an end in Western Europe.

It is significant that it was in America, the first and greatest union of states, that the transnational company was born; and the briefest look at American politics is enough to prove beyond doubt that in a very large state the very large company will never lack political influence and will never be easily tamed.

In summary, the big markets and big companies have their place and can, when rightly used, contribute greatly to our prosperity. They also have their dangers and their ill-effects, and in attempting to avoid them it is fatal to put our trust in large political unions within which individual states have lost the power to control their own economies. The test-bed on which this is being worked out today is the European Union. We are assured by the lovers of size that any European nation state that does not enter the embrace of the Union is doomed to be marginalised, to eke out a precarious existence that will inevitably end in decline while the members of the Union surge on towards a glorious future. It can be made to sound very convincing until one comes to look at the facts, and the facts are that small countries such as Switzerland, Iceland and even Liechtenstein are proving to be considerably more prosperous than countries inside the European Union. When the people of Norway voted against membership of the European Union, the Union's supporters gleefully predicted that this ill-advised country would soon be forced to change its mind by the impoverishment that must inevitably overtake it. The years have gone by, and Norway is doing outstandingly well. It must be intensely irritating for the prophets of doom. And what a contrast to Sweden!

Outside Europe, countries that are far smaller than Britain, such as New Zealand, retain their independence, trade throughout the world, and do very well out of it. And there is one country above all which shows how to prosper by exploiting world-wide markets while remaining a separate, self-contained and highly individualistic nation state. Japan is a big country compared to Norway but it is small compared to Europe as a whole. Is there anyone who thinks he can persuade the Japanese that they would be better off if they gave up their independent sovereignty and merged in a Pacific Union with everyone from Malaysia to Tonga? Japan succeeds because, among other things, she has great self-confidence. Britain went into 'Europe' largely because she had lost hers. The Empire was gone and British industry was in decline, crippled by lethargic management and by the restrictive practices of belligerent trade unions. The British looked with respect and envy at the German 'economic miracle' and hoped that, if they linked themselves closely to the Continental countries, efficiency would prove to be catching. Britain has now cured many of her own ills and is in a position to benefit from independence. It would be very sad if, just when she had reached that point, she lost that opportunity and merged herself in a centralised federal state. The damage would be all the greater because those who control that state are the true believers in an obsolete faith, whose central doctrine is that in business and politics bigger is always better.

3

War and Peace

It is clear, then, that many of the economic benefits claimed for large states and federations turn out to be illusory when they are subjected to a closer examination. However, those who believe that big is beautiful have another position to fall back on. Nation states, they assert, have always gone to war with each other, and unless they are restrained by some larger authority they will go on doing so. In particular federalists claim that it is the European Union, in its present and earlier forms, that has saved us from the outbreak of a fourth Franco-German war.

To anyone who remembers the 1930s and the totally different atmosphere of European politics at that time this seems a strange idea. Since the end of the Second World War there has never been the sense of imminent conflict that haunted the inter-war years and, though there have been wars in Europe, all of them have been within states, not between them. Yugoslavia has broken up. The USSR has been broken up. Russia itself has splintered and some of its component 'republics' have fought for independence. Northern Ireland has seen almost continuous bloodshed for nearly thirty years. In Cyprus, Greeks and Turks have been in conflict, but it is significant that, although Greece and Turkey have made warlike noises, they have not gone to war with each other as they might easily have done in an earlier period of history.

Various possible explanations have been put forward for this outbreak of international peace. One is that after 1945 the real threat of war came from the USSR, and under the shadow of a mighty neighbour armed with nuclear weapons, the nations of Western Europe were more likely to huddle together defensively than to start fighting each other.

Another explanation sees the cause of wars between economically developed countries as a particular stage of capitalist development. Marxist historians hold that as a capitalist economy expands it encounters an inevitable shortfall in the purchasing power of its consumers. As a result the state concerned starts to pursue protectionist policies. In a capitalist system, Marx maintained, employers must retain some profits from the price they received for their goods. The sum total of all wages in the economy will therefore never equal the value of all the goods and services that are supplied, and as the aggregate of wage-earners is almost the same as the aggregate of consumers, there will be a crisis in which the market cannot absorb what is produced. Capitalists have no wish to share an already inadequate home market with outsiders. But any form of protection has an adverse effect on the industries of other countries. They retaliate, a conflict of interest occurs, and this soon escalates. Mutual recrimination is followed by something like economic warfare and in the end this may lead to a real shooting war.

The second effect of the crisis is the quest for colonies, which the capitalists need to provide a captive market for their products and also as a source of cheap raw materials. The rush by the European powers to colonise more than half the human race began in the early years of the capitalist system and by the end of the nineteenth-century they had run out of people to colonise. Gaining another colony meant taking someone else's and this led to the world wars of the twentieth-century. Germany, as a late comer in the race for colonies, became the prime aggressor. Since the 1940s, of course, the process of colonisation has been reversed, so this source of conflict has been removed and Europe has been at peace. We now know that this argument to show that capitalist states inevitably go to war with each other does not hold water. The mechanism proposed by Marx by which such states were bound to outgrow their own markets does not in fact operate. The money retained by an employer or distributed as dividends is not lost to the economy. A very few people may hoard their banknotes under the mattress but every other pound keeps circulating. The employer who retains part of the profit achieves nothing unless that money is spent, whether on new machinery, new buildings, research, or whatever. The fallacy in the Marxist argument should be rather obvious, but it has not prevented many socialists from embracing federalism as a policy for achieving peace.

26

States can reach a steady state of prosperity without being imperial powers, particularly if they trade with each other. They need not even be large states, as the high standard of living in small countries today amply demonstrates.

The example of the small state also refutes the belief that ideology will give rise to international conflict. Fascism and Communism are obvious examples, and the big states who embraced these creeds were certainly aggressive. This was not true, however, of the smaller ones. Spain under Franco was Falangist (not quite the same thing as Italy's Fascism but recognisably similar) but she showed no aggressive tendencies to other nations. Throughout the Second World War Spain and Portugal, also a dictatorship with fascist sympathies, not only remained neutral but turned a blind-eye to Allied operations within their territories that they could easily have frustrated.

Whatever theory one may hold about the particular causes of war, there is one fact that can be accepted without argument. There would be no wars if human beings were not by nature capable of aggressiveness. Their aggressiveness becomes more marked when they band together in groups, by race, or by nation, and we have seen terrible examples of this in Yugoslavia, Rwanda, and elsewhere. The Indians are generally regarded as gentle people but millions died in the ferocious massacres by Hindus and Moslems against each other at the time of independence. Among Europeans, the Portuguese may be as kindly as any, but in their empire building they were unutterably cruel to a subject people. We scarcely associate any of the Scandinavians with militaristic instincts, but Danes, Swedes, and Norwegians were once ruthless to their enemies in other lands. As for the Germans, meet them today and you cannot believe their fathers behaved as they did half a century ago.

Once again the lust for power seems to be behind this. People whose personal lives may be unsatisfying, constrained and full of petty frustrations can glory in being the citizens of a big and powerful state. The cotton-picker in Mississippi or the clerk in downtown Chicago can feel proud of Uncle Sam as the Sixth Fleet sails out to quell some trouble as the world's policeman. An earlier British generation could have similar feelings when they looked at an atlas and saw a quarter of the world's land surface coloured red and learned as schoolchildren that England had never lost a war. No doubt the Romans felt like this, and the French before Napoleon fell. Certainly the Germans did under Hitler, and it was the promise of this intoxicating sense of mass strength that brought him to power.

Today the European Union is beginning to re-ignite such feelings. It is to have a population of 350 million, making it the largest superstate in the West and with a wealth greater than that of the United States. It will be able to afford the largest and best equipped armed forces. It will be a state of immense power, more powerful than any in history. If the argument of this book is valid, the edifice will collapse before this great concentration of power is seen, but the dream is cherished by many and even now it affords pride and a little arrogance among the dreamers in Brussels.

The examples of aggressiveness that we have looked at show that it is not the nation state as such that is the cause of war. Groups within states fight each other. Federations and unions such as the USA and the old USSR are no less belligerent. Could we trust ourselves to be pacifist if Europe ever became a military superpower? One generalisation we can make is that it is often an imbalance of forces that triggers a war. The more powerful state makes war on the less powerful, which responds by trying to increase its power and retaliate.

The history of France and Germany provides an example. At the beginning of the nineteenth-century France was the continent's greatest power. Her population was smaller than Russia's but her economic capacity for warfare was stronger. In contrast, Austria had had the largest army in Europe in the seventeenth and eighteenth-centuries, but had fallen to fifth place by the nineteenth. During the twenty-five-year period when France was overtaking Austria to have the largest continental army, she invaded Germany no less than twelve times. The first invasion was in 1792, the twelfth in 1813. The unification of Germany began in 1815 and it can be clearly seen as a response to the threat from France, when she began to rearm soon after the Napoleonic wars were over. Why would the princelings, archdukes, and dukes of those little German states have given up their independence except to gain security? If in the twentieth-century the French have feared a powerful and united Germany it is because the Germans once feared the French.

This should convince us that the competitive banding together of small states to form large ones is not a recipe for peace. A major war is much less likely in a continent of small states especially if each is of much the same size and strength as the others. As things are now, we have to live with the existence of superstates, but the cause of peace will be much better served by doing what we can to persuade those superstates to devolve their power downwards and to encourage a degree of independence in their constituent parts than it will by building up one more rival superstate.

A case in point is the break-up of the USSR. In seeking their independence, some of the republics, such as Chechnya, have resorted to armed force, but once that independence is gained they are no threat to the outside world. Estonia, Latvia, and Lithuania have won their liberty and their status as nation states. Having applauded their bravery, are we now fearful of what they may do?

For some years it has become fashionable to decry the nation state. Many politicians, academics, media pundits, and others fail to see the inconsistency of welcoming the transformation of colonies into self-governing and sovereign peoples and their disdain for the nation state since the two are one and the same. Plead the cause of the nation state and you are likely to be treated with disdain, as if you had failed to comprehend a self-evident truth. It is interesting, though, that the fashion is less among the young than amid the middle-aged and elderly who remember the Second World War and its aftermath. What they see in the nation state is its power to declare war. What they fail to see is its power to cooperate. In the modern world no country, however large, is an island to itself. It is obliged at the least to trade with others and even the biggest states have sought to cooperate with others. No example is more obvious that that of the United States as a member of NATO and the North American Free Trade Association with Mexico and Canada. There are many ways in which a country can integrate informally with others without surrendering its sovereignty, and it is those that we should be exploring. If in future the world is able to escape from war and the threat of war that has plagued it since civilisation began, it will not be because it has organised itself into a few huge power blocs. It will be because many independent nations have learned to cooperate, and above all, to trade freely with each other, enjoying the prosperity that this can bring and having no wish to exchange it for the destruction and poverty that is the inevitable consequence of war.

4

The Disease of Growth

It is a sad paradox of our times that as we have grown richer the amount of crime in our society, so far from diminishing, has sharply increased. This is true throughout most of Western Europe and it is true in the even more affluent United States of America. The Victorians believed that crime was a result of poverty. If people are desperate from hunger and destitution, as many then were, some of them are going to steal or turn violent. Therefore, as society grows wealthier and even the poor are less poverty-stricken surely crime will lessen? It seemed a reasonable belief and yet today we lock our doors and windows, shops install elaborate and expensive surveillance equipment to frustrate thieves, we guard our children on their way to school, and many of us are afraid to walk the streets at night. What has gone wrong?

Plainly there are a host of immediate reasons why someone steals, rapes, or murders, but when a whole society becomes markedly more prone to crime we must look for general causes. A number have been suggested, but there is one that is clearly established and that is directly relevant to the theme of this book: crime generally is on a vastly greater scale in the largest states of Europe – in Britain, France, Germany and Italy, in particular – than in the smaller ones, just as it is worse in large cities than in small communities. In Iceland there is virtually no crime, though it has a population similar in size to a large city in Britain. Norway, too, with a population about half that of London, seems to be immune from the wave of criminal aggression. The same can be said of all the smaller countries outside the European Union.

One obvious reason why we would expect crime rates to be lower in small communities of all kinds is that in them crime and criminals are much more visible. It is not easy to get away with robbery or violence when you and your victim are well known to everyone around you, and when retribution is administered by people close at hand. It is this that produces the urge towards vigilantism in people who feel that the justice system is too remote to protect them. We hear continually about the tenants of some estate whose lives are made wretched by a few teenage boys vandalising the buildings and frightening the more vulnerable residents. The tenants know perfectly well who they are but the police and the courts seem powerless to stop them. However much one may disapprove of private people taking the law into their own hands, one has to admit that if that estate were a self-contained political unit the trouble-makers would soon be given short shrift.

There is also a connection, though a less obvious one, between the size of a community and the most important reason for rising rates of crime. To understand this, one needs to ask not why crime is common but why it is not universal. Why is not every teenager a criminal? After all, smashing windows and stealing videos is a lot more fun than sitting quietly in school learning French irregular verbs, and it can be rather more profitable, at least in the short-term.

The fear of punishment is only part of the answer. Most petty crimes are never brought home to the perpetrator and the criminal knows that the chance of his being convicted of any one particular crime is vanishingly small. What keeps most of us out of crime is a commonly-accepted social morality. To us the idea of going out and committing a burglary is simply unthinkable, and so long as this remains the consensus among the great majority of people in a community, crime will be held within bounds.

For various reasons that consensus has been breaking down in western societies. We see this in every walk of life. It is not just the delinquent youth whose misbehaviour is accepted by his peers. In the city, two generations ago, a financier found guilty of fraud would have been shunned for life. Now he is welcomed back into the boardroom.

This process had deep historic roots. In part it can be seen as a result of the emphasis on individual rights that has been dominant in modern times. For centuries after the Norman conquest England was an authoritarian state, and the emphasis in feudal society was not on rights but on duties. The serf had a duty to serve the baron and in return the baron had a duty to protect those beneath him, but with the movement from medieval to modern society all this changed.

If the old order of feudalism placed too much power in the hands of the few, and was inevitably abused and corrupted, the rise of a mercantile class in Western Europe made its demise certain. In the new society the emphasis shifted away from social ties towards personal rights and freedoms, and from John Locke onwards Europe's philosophers began to accentuate the worth of the individual as against the power of the state. A century later Voltaire was proclaiming this message in France and it was spread throughout the world by the English, American and French revolutions.

The inter-war years of the twentieth century brought the great totalitarian reaction, but since the Second World War the liberal tradition has returned to Germany and Italy and is taking over in Russia. It is now the dominant philosophy throughout Europe and it is noteworthy that Monnet, Schuman, Adenauer, Spaak and the others who were major influences in the earlier days of the European Economic Community had read and endorsed the moral and political beliefs of John Locke, Jeremy Bentham and John Stuart Mill, as well as others of the liberal school on the Continent, and were anxious that the new order for Western Europe should be in accord with those beliefs. It was a tribute to English philosophy and a reason why the more idealistic of the Community's architects were disappointed that Britain did not sign the Treaty of Rome at the outset.

We are now seeing the emphasis on rights becoming exaggerated in various ways, some of which are grotesque. In America, and now in Europe, the legal profession has exploded to cope with a torrent of claims of every sort and kind. When a women who spills hot coffee on her own legs she can successfully sue the company that supplied her with the coffee, it is clear that a liberal belief in freedom has been pushed and twisted into something its proponents never intended.

To some extent this new attitude is born of a softness of character among a generation most of whom, uniquely in human history, have never known the horrors of war or the pinch of hunger and poverty. Their complaints have become more strident precisely because they have had so little to complain about. It may be a good thing that those who are still poor are conscious of their rights and that there are pressure groups to uphold them, but this in itself is a reaction to the perversion of liberal economics embodied in a *laissez-faire* society in which the strong are

33

liberated to get stronger and the very rich to get richer, while the weakest are left to the devil.

Unfetter man's egotism and there will be no limit to what he may desire, and in the modern world there is seemingly no end to the things available to those who can stretch out their hands far enough. Material goods are the most obvious target, and as the resources of our planet are finite it is going to be difficult to accommodate the demands of the West, let alone allow the four or five billion people elsewhere to catch up and have an equal share. Yet the right to an ever-rising standard of living is, in most people's minds, unquestioned. Our neighbour has a new car, a video, a swimming pool, or an exotic holiday, so we ought to have one too. When we reflect that we work as hard as he does, the 'ought' becomes a moral right, and in time many such rights become blessed by law. The clamour goes on: the right to a house, even to a child, is on the statute book of one country after another in the West, and before long the moral right to a job may have the force of law.

The quest for rights goes beyond material things. The right to 'the pursuit of happiness', enshrined in the American constitution, is echoed in other countries. Quite what it implies has never been made clear and in many people's minds it becomes simply a right to happiness: if I am unhappy I have a moral right to expect the rest of society to make amends. Absurd though it is, this proposition can be heard in surprising places; to disagree, it will not be enough to repeat Aristotle: "Happiness depends upon ourselves."

This clamour for rights has offended both the Left and the Right. Their philosophers are starting to rethink their ideas, and this is happening particularly on the Left following the collapse of authoritarian socialism in the Soviet bloc. A sense of duty is being asserted. Foremost in this new schools of thinking is David Selbourne, whose *Principle of Duty*, published in 1994, is having a profound influence on ethical and political thought. He is far from being alone among his contemporaries but in recent years none has expressed this dilemma of morals with such logical vehemence or lucid coherence.

To Selbourne, what is important is the civic order. This does not simply mean the state, for the state with all its arms – government, legislature, police, law courts, army, and so forth – is only a part of the civic order, which is ultimately a moral relationship. Selbourne identifies three circles of relationships by which every member of the human race is circumscribed. The first two circles are the family and the community in which we live and work. It is not, as a rule, obligatory for us to belong to one community, for if we feel ill-at-ease or think we can do better for ourselves elsewhere, most of us are free to move on to another community. The third circle, on which the civic order is based, is the state into which we are born or to which we migrate. This, says Selbourne, is a nation or city of determinate size that is self-governing and therefore sovereign, with an aggregate of citizens with determinate rights, duties, privileges and benefits, and an institutional coherence. Within this state Selbourne emphasises the need for the development of a 'civic bond'. He defines this as the ethic voluntarily assumed by the citizen, but sustained by law, which governs the relations between the individuals comprising the civil order as citizens and teaches them that they are members of one and the same civil order. The civil bond also teaches them that they are bound by a principle of duty and that each has a responsibility for the well-being of all in the civil order.

This is moral health, in the older meaning of the word. There can be no civil bond or civil order if society is no more than a mass of people who happen to live in the same area but do not share the same moral values. Moreover a citizen is not, as Selbourne puts it, "a mere bundle of rights which may be asserted against the civil area". Anyone choosing to live within a civil order who fails to accept the civil bond is deemed a moral stranger, for the civil order is based on morality and the state is its 'arm and instrument'.

This clearly implies a need for a strong moral consensus within the state, and it is obvious that this is easier to attain in small states than in large ones. It is absent in the largest countries of the world today and even in a country the size of Britain the desire of many Scottish and Welsh people for devolution or independence shows a longing for a degree of unity and coherence that they do not feel in the present United Kingdom.

There are those who take a contrary view to Selbourne's and who believe that any grouping of men and women will, given time, settle down to a reasonable state of co-existence, especially if aided by a full dose of religion. This is looking increasingly over-optimistic, and though one cannot deny that religion has had a benign effect on the morals of countless millions it cannot, on its own, be relied on to sustain the civil order. It is significant that in the fundamentalist countries of our own time, religion is very much a vehicle for proclaiming national or cultural identity; in a country such as Iran it is a whole traditional way of life that is being asserted. It is also significant that its rulers feel the need to support religious doctrine with a penal code of extreme severity. In contrast, it is difficult to foresee our Parliament decreeing that as the Church of England had failed to ensure a law-abiding society all criminals would be beheaded, flogged or stoned to death.

The most draconian punishments are ineffective if criminals are not caught, and they will not be caught if those around them feel helpless or passive in the face of crime and disorder, or if they do not feel any strong disapproval. Many people are quite indifferent to shop-lifting from a big supermarket but would be shocked by theft from a corner shop. When we come to crime on a Europe-wide scale our tolerance is extraordinary. We know that the Common Agricultural Policy is ravaged by frauds; each year about six billion pounds are siphoned off by crooks, mostly traders in surplus foods. This estimate comes from the Court of Auditors and is the minimum figure! It represents about a quarter of all the money allocated in assisting the farming community in Western Europe which, put another way, could give the poorest five per cent of the people in the European Union about £300 each – almost £1,000 a year for a family of three, enough to transform their lives. Are we horrified? The media report this as a minor item of news; there is no backlash from an aggrieved public; in Britain there may be a question or two in the House but elsewhere the response is muted. Just suppose that fraud on this scale were committed year after year in Britain! There would be a furious outcry, the tabloids would scream, newscasters would grimace at the camera, there would be debates in Parliament, Ministers would be called on to resign, and urgent steps would be taken to end the scandal. Meanwhile in bars and bus queues, in factory canteens and railway carriages, a clamour would be raised. Ordinary people would feel that, even if they could not do anything directly, something would in the end be done if enough voices called for it loudly enough. They would be demonstrating that in Britain the civil bond does still draw us together, although only just. As British citizens people are morally active; as Europeans the same people are morally passive.

This weakening of the civic bond as political units grow larger explains more than anything else why crime is so much less prevalent in small countries. A small nation that is culturally and linguistically united, such as Iceland or Norway, will down the generations have evolved a broadly-accepted approach to moral questions. The laws are understood and obeyed because they have been made in accordance with the will of the people. It is also true that in a small nation the coercion of law plays a smaller part, since every citizen accepts responsibility for the well-being of the whole, and the criminal code is only needed to deal with the few black sheep that are to be found in even the smallest country. What keeps the great majority of citizens on an honest course is their understanding that they have duties as well as rights and that they can only have the benefits of the civil order if they accept the civil bond.

In theory this is what is supposed to happen in any democracy: the people choose their rulers and will therefore be willing to obey the laws they make. In reality that is far from the truth in most countries throughout the world. People do not feel that they are taking part in the governing process, and there is a sense in which they are obviously right. How much real influence can any one citizen exert by casting his single vote once every four or five years along with fifty, a hundred, perhaps five or six hundred million others? This is true in the most fair and democratic country and even in such countries elections are too often fought on dubious promises that make the elector's choice a sham. The bigger the electorate the less effective the vote, and this futility is not lost on the people in US presidential elections, when only about half the electorate make the effort to go down to the polling booth.

In every country purporting to be a democracy there is evidence of such disillusionment. If this grows the ground is fertilised for some kind of totalitarian rule. Even as things are, the phrase 'elective dictatorship' has entered the language; and not unfairly, for as soon as a party leader has been elected as head of the government for a period of years he or she effectively governs without the people's consent, and the larger the majority at the last election the less heed needs to be paid to any voice that demurs.

One result of this sense of alienation from the ordinary political process is that people who do want to make some impression band together not in political parties but in pressure groups. In the last fifty years a great many of these have sprung up and some of them exercise considerable influence. Broadly, they are of two kinds. One sort are the successors of the trade associations and other bodies speaking for various industries and professional interests; the other sort campaign for what they see as altruistic ends, such as the environment, animal welfare, or consumer protection. Often the two sorts come into conflict. If a new motorway is being planned you are likely to find the Road Haulage Federation campaigning vigorously for it to go ahead while Friends of the Earth campaign just as vigorously to have it stopped.

The first influence of these groups lies in their ability to feed stories to the media. Newspaper editors and television producers are always glad to know of new subjects, especially if they are likely to arouse strong feelings, for or against, in their readers and viewers. When public interest has been aroused, the next step is to lobby the civil service and members of Parliament. Civil servants are seldom backward in extending their empire and MPs will bow to the views of a sufficient number of voters.

In London alone are the offices of over two hundred of these pressure groups. Many have their counterparts in most of the capitals of the European Union, while in Washington their number is believed to be still greater. Collectively it all adds up to a powerful force, and it has to be said that the best of these groups have alerted the public to real abuses and dangers and have done much to remedy them. On the other hand it is also true that a well-financed pressure group, whether it aims to further the interests of its members or speaks for what it believes to be the general good, can exert an influence far greater than that of individual citizens and is therefore in danger of being a minority imposing its will on the majority; and that members of that majority will continue to feel that they have no real influence over the forces that rule their lives.

To speak of a 'silent majority' is something of a cliché, but when the silence of a majority grows to sullen resentment, as it naturally will sooner or later, disenchantment with the democratic process follows. Democracy works when majorities elect their representatives and they govern with the continued confidence of the majority. One way that confidence can be lost is when the majority realises its elected representatives are submitting to undue pressure from minorities. Pressure groups would be unnecessary if their views were those already held by the majority, so by their very nature they speak for minorities. While it is absolutely right that a minority should try to persuade the majority, it is another matter altogether when the minority, having formed a pressure group, by-passes a democratic campaign among the majority and concentrates its efforts upon the government itself. Yet in a large state this is the obvious strategy. The larger the population the more difficult it is for the newly-formed pressure group, with limited funds and a modest membership, to get its message across. If the population is very small, the problem does not arise, and a professionally-organised and highly-funded pressure organisation is not necessary. In New Zealand a single individual operating from his home at little expense can run an effective campaign about national issues: the smaller the crowd, the smaller the voice need be. No one in that small country need feel cut-off from the democratic process. Although majority opinion is almost certainly going to prevail, a handful of New Zealanders can convert their minority into a majority. That is, of course, as it should be, but it can only happen if the democratic process operates on a human scale. And that becomes impossible once the population goes beyond a very few million. Norway and Sweden in the past have had a similar governance, but that is no longer so, as the Swedes are beginning to realise to their regret. One stops at Oslo; the other may go on to Brussels and get lost.

The larger the population of a state – and the European Union is already extremely large – the more impotent a minority becomes, and the individual voice goes unheard. Even in the political parties democracy breaks down: the larger the state, the more necessary they become, but as the party grows in size, so not only the individual member but also large minorities must give way to a still greater number. And such mass majorities tend to be swayed emotionally rather than rationally. Pressure groups know this, so do the tabloid editors and television producers. By influencing the latter, the pressure group can exert pressure on the general public – a mass majority – who in turn will persuade a majority within a political party to adopt the views of the pressure group. That they too have been influenced emotionally rather than rationally (and one of the emotions is hope of electoral success by gaining the support of the pressure group) does little to further the broader interest of the general population.

The pressure groups seem to be a device of the Western democracies, but mega-states such as India and Indonesia have shown that they too can be elective dictatorships where governments can flout majority opinion. In any country large enough, many things can be done by a government against the wishes of their people, for leaders may have their own agendas, which are not necessarily the same as their election manifestos, and they will have their own supporters and fund-suppliers to placate. There are several reasons why a governing party can behave in this way and the larger the state the greater the opportunity for it to do so. The bigger the government, the more patronage it will have to distribute, and it will be singularly inept if it fails to use such power to its own advantage. Because a modern government in Western Europe interfaces with almost every branch of human activity, it can please its supporters with lots of minor offices besides those at the centre of government. People who join the rank and file of a political party may have no ambitions for themselves, but those who climb up the ladder will have one eye on the fruits of office. In lots of ways, some more subtle than others, the party machine can coax the doubters to support the elective dictatorship. It can, after all, be rather nice to be invited to a special dinner party or merely consulted by the leader himself.

The media are less malleable, and although they may strike some strident blows upon the government, they can be manipulated none the less. Professor F. A. Hayek, in his *The Road to Serfdom* half a century ago, spelt out how an interventionist government can acquire an undue influence over the media. Because governments are making news every day they can manage how it is presented, for journalists seldom have either the time or the expense allowance to enable them to gather all the information their readers expect. I once had lunch with the diplomatic correspondent of a famous newspaper. He confessed that he had done no work that morning; in fact, after a good party the night before, he had only just got out of bed in time to come to our rendezvous. At three o'clock I ventured that he might be late for work. "Not a bit of it," he assured me. "Being a diplomatic correspondent is the easiest job in the world. The Foreign Office will send down all the news I want and in half an hour I can write my copy." Like his colleagues he knew facts given by the government's press office would be accurate but might not tell the whole story, and they would lead him to draw a conclusion favourable to the government. Besides, the other diplomatic correspondents would report the same facts so the rival papers would not contradict him.

Paradoxically, the coming of television, which has brought political news into every home, has also served to distance the electorate from its rulers. I stood for parliament in 1950, once in a general election and once in a by-election, and again in 1951 and 1955. The first time I saw a television set was when I was visiting a supporter during the general election of 1951. There was probably no more than a handful of sets in the whole constituency and they were of no political significance, but in those four election campaigns there were two, three, sometimes four meetings every evening and all of them were well attended. Supporters came to support, opponents to oppose and heckle, and the marginal voters to make up their minds. Every speech had to be carefully constructed, a single word could raise a heckle, and if the candidate failed to shine his supporters would go home disheartened, opponents elated and marginal voters put off. In the 1997 General Election, like many candidates I did not hold a single public meeting. If democracy is about accountability, I certainly was not accountable for what I had done as I had been in the 1950's.

It is television that has brought about this change and the trouble is that television is a one-way medium. The viewer can see and hear the politician – or rather a carefully presented image of him – but the politician can neither see nor hear the elector, who has no way of making

40

his opinions known. Newspapers are not in that position; their editors know that they cannot afford to ignore their correspondence columns and that editorial comment must accord with readers' views or circulation will fall. When Balfour described democracy as 'government by explanation' he may have been right at the time: a politician then explained himself to an audience that could respond and often did so *fortissimo*. In the age of television Balfour's words have become sadly out of date.

If people feel that they have no power to change things they soon lose interest. I often find the political opinions of my constituents, especially those under thirty, monosyllabic. If you feel your views count for nothing in influencing the decisions that govern your life, the effort to formulate them logically and state them lucidly becomes rather a pointless exercise.

This sense of alienation can be very dangerous. What starts as apathy can turn into something a great deal nastier. Adler in *Understanding Human Nature* divided men and women into submissive and imperious types. He went on, "the servile individual lives by the rules and laws of others, and this type seeks out a servile position almost compulsively." The danger is that when such people become frustrated and angry enough at their inability to control their own lives, the organisations to which they submit themselves will be those that offer a service not just of comradeship but of power. Privates in the army enjoy a sense of security, because they are part of a large institution that will look after them and provide for their needs in return for obedience. They can also feel pride in their regiment's past victories and in the knowledge that they are part of a mighty armed force that stands ready to defeat its enemies once again. Submission has brought a kind of corporate dominance.

It was an extreme form of this process that brought Hitler to power and it is at work in the fundamentalist regimes of the modern world. Because it is a basic human response it can never cease to be a danger and it is always a greater danger in large countries and empires. The larger the state the smaller any one individual or group must loom in it, and also the less the government will be able to accommodate itself to the diversity of interests, opinions and desires within it. In the mega-state the sense of powerlessness descends on even the most articulate minority. In a democracy minorities must give way to majorities but as the state grows so do minorities. Tens of millions of people have to accept that their lives must be controlled by the interests of others who are still more numerous. Sitting behind a desk in Brussels hundreds of miles from most of the peoples of Europe, the European Union commissioner, like any other mandarin of a mega-state has to make a decision that will be binding on a

41

whole population. How can he possibly assess the effect on all the diverse millions of people who will be bound by it? The most he can do is to construct in his mind some sort of average figure, like the 'reference man' devised by the United Nations Food and Agricultural Organisation. ('Reference man' is aged twenty five, weighs sixty-five kilograms, spends eight hours a day working, eight hours sleeping and eight hours otherwise occupied. His work and recreation require moderate activity and he lives in a climate neither too hot nor too cold.) This may be a useful concept in determining how much food our world needs to produce but it works very badly in politics. How many of us conform to reference man?

The larger and more heterogeneous the population, the more laws are needed to regulate the infinite number of conflicting interests; but the greater their number the more minorities will have to change their ways to comply with them and so lose their freedom as individuals. For laws to be truly just they must be for a homogeneous people.

The dilemma is, paradoxically, more acute in an advanced democracy then in a primitive dictatorship. Mao could assume that the millions of peasants in the China of his day shared one overriding desire: to get enough of life's necessities to survive. The imposition of common standards would not be irksome; if they all rode the same sort of bicycles and lived in the same sort of dwellings that would be a price worth paying. But no such assumption could be made in an affluent democratic country. People have been encouraged to pursue diverse activities and to make diverse choices, and inevitably one person's choices will conflict with another's.

This presents an impossible task to the politician or civil servant in considering the interests of the average man; and at the bottom, the whole idea of an average human being is meaningless. What is the average of a greengrocer and a musician? You can, of course, take averages of such quantifiable things as age and income, but when you have done so how much does it help? Is it a good idea to treat a seventy-year-old women living on a her state pension and a thirty-year-old commodity broker with an annual income of a quarter of a million as if they were each an average being aged fifty and earning £127,000?

Every state inevitably finds itself imposing some degree of homogeneity. The larger the state the more that becomes true and the more irrelevant the homogeneous pattern becomes to many of the citizens. This process can be seen hard at work in the European Union as the amount of legislation grows to immense proportions and has to be applied to the concept of an average European. Can somebody explain what would be the average of a Greek's and a Swede's desires from life and what relevance it would have to either of them?

The problem of homogeneity arises not just within states but between them. In a world of many small independent countries there will be a diversity of styles and systems. The people in each state will see the blessings or drawbacks of the others and in a modern world of easy travel many of them will have first-hand experience of what life is like across the frontiers. It was a process of this kind that contributed significantly to the downfall of the Communist dictatorship in Russia. Despite restrictions on travel and control of the media it was impossible for the government to prevent word getting around that the working classes in capitalist democracies were not starving in the streets but in fact enjoyed many things the Russian people were eager to enjoy for themselves.

That sort of enlightenment can only occur in a world where a diverging of systems exists, and that is one good reason why we should resist the impulse to impose our own system on other peoples. Britain could be described as a meritocratic constitutional monarchy and parliamentary democracy with a semi-interventionist form of capitalism. Of all the countries in the world there is only a handful that conforms to that description: the vast majority of people have chosen not to follow Britain's example, and they are absolutely entitled to make their own choices.

In the mega-state they cannot do so. The countries included in it must abandon their different traditions and accept they will, to a greater or lesser degree, be ruled in ways that are alien to them. To the extent that that happens there is bound to be a weakening of people's sense that they are freely participating in their own self-government. When that sense is lost there is a loosening of the civil bond on which all democratic order depends. All mega-states are diseased because their peoples cannot be at ease within them.

5

Bring on the Artist

One major problem that arises from treating human beings as if they were averages is that those who conform to the average are seldom the most valuable or enterprising. In particular, those who are truly creative in science and the arts are very far from average. It is interesting to look at the societies in which art, philosophy, and science have flourished to see if we can discern any common factors.

For a start, it is clear that peace and stable prosperity are not necessities. The greatest flowering of English literature happened during the Elizabethan age, a time of violence, instability, religious quarrel,s and the threat of war. The seventeenth century saw continuing discord culminating in civil war – and saw also the birth of the scientific revolution in the work of Newton and his fellows, following on from the work of Galileo in an equally discordant Italy that had produced the stupendous achievements of the Renaissance. The English novel reached its greatest flowering in the Victorian era, when revolutionary social and economic changes were threatening to tear society apart. Above all, in the city states of ancient Greece, philosophy (and many would say drama, sculpture, and architecture too) rose to heights of achievement that have never been topped in all the centuries since. As one distinguished professor of philosophy put it, all our new thoughts are but footnotes to the script of the Athenians. Yet the fifth and sixth centuries B.C. were not times of classical tranquillity: there were constant inter-city wars, famine, revolution, and the looming threat of the mighty Persian empire.

Incidentally, all this is very discouraging for those who hope that literature, philosophy, and the arts in general will exert a civilising influence and, along with religion, help to tame the aggressiveness of modern society. Whatever their effect in refining individual human minds, there is no evidence that the arts produce social or international peace. When peace did come to the ancient Mediterranean it was not as a result of anything the philosophers had said: it was imposed by the militantly expanding forces of Rome.

Another fallacy is to suppose that because the arts can only flourish where there is enough wealth to support them, they will flourish most in big cities and states which have a higher total wealth than small ones. In reality what matters is not the totality of wealth but the sense, at least in a particular part or class of society, that it is well enough off to afford to take an interest in artistic and intellectual achievement. Since, in general, small states are more prosperous *per capita* than big states, they are more likely to provide a fertile ground for any such achievement.

Artists and thinkers tend to gather at centres of excellence, but the absolute size of those centres is unimportant. In fifth-century B.C. Athens the number of free citizens (that is, excluding slaves) was less than one third of the population of present-day Brighton. What matters is the place that society accords to intellectual activities in its order of priorities, and here the small state scores again. Not only must big states spend a larger proportion of their resources on administration (this point is discussed in Chapter 6) but in any large country the business of organising society goes far beyond the work of civil servants. Pressure groups, professional bodies, trade associations, trade unions, political parties multiply in a large state – all these organisations can contain literally millions of people, and the people who join them must have less time, energy, and enthusiasm to give to any artistic or cultural pursuit.

Another problem with today's capital cities as centres of excellence is that they have become much less attractive places to live in. The art galleries, the concert halls and opera houses, the principal publishers and literary agents are still to be found there, but the creative artists and their patrons are moving out of New York, London, Paris, and Rome to the outer suburbs and beyond, where streets are freer of traffic and safer to walk along, where schools for their children are better and the air is fresher, and where a writer does not have to be among the tiny company of best-sellers to afford a house.

The basic truth is that, like all delicate growths, creative work of all kinds only flourishes in a congenial environment. The society in which it takes place must put a high value on it and that will not be so in societies that are dedicated to the pursuit of power. Since it is the pursuit of power that gives rise to large-scale institutions, we can see why it is more often in small societies that the arts have flourished. The Roman empire was far bigger, richer, more peaceful, and better managed than the squabbling collection of Greek city states a few centuries earlier. It was the natural product of a mentality that valued order and authority (imposed, of course, by the exercise of power); yet in comparison with the disorderly Greeks, its intellectual contribution was negligible. Art, architecture, drama, music, philosophy, and political thought – the subjects on which Aristotle, Plato, and their contemporaries had placed such emphasis – gave way to the utilitarian. Law, engineering, and military science must take their place when it comes to building empires, settling colonies, and keeping quiet a conquered people.

Centuries later it was England's turn to build an even greater empire, yet before the empire-builders went forth, what a burst of artistic activity there was in England. Here was a country with a population of no more than four million, with London a tiny fraction of its present size. Yet there were more than twice the number of theatres than today in the capital and they were filled for more performances as they put on plays by Shakespeare, Marlowe, Ben Johnson, and many lesser playwrights. Music, too, reached a peak of excellence and was played and sung not just by professionals but by ordinary people in their own homes. The expansion of English power began and the lute was put away in favour of sterner work. By the time England reached the heyday of her wealth and imperial power her theatres were showing crude Victorian melodramas, and the only music she produced that is still played was in the comedies of Gilbert and Sullivan or the bombastic notes of Elgar, both a mirror of the age.

Pre-Bismarckian Germany was also a scene of cultural ferment. The little states and principalities abounded with artists, writers, musicians, playwrights, architects, and philosophers. Bach, Mozart, Beethoven, Nietzsche, Herine, Kant, Schopenhauer, Duever, and Holbein have all had an impact on Western culture unsurpassed by any German since the Prussian Empire gave her people other tasks to do. Travelling through the heartland of Europe today one is struck by the glory, and still more by the diversity, of its architecture. It is not most of the modern buildings that catch one's eye, but the houses, churches, cathedrals, theatres, opera houses, town halls, and castles that were built before the unification of Germany. As you go from one of the former little states to the next you encounter different styles, varying materials, a changing ambience. Some are quietly elegant, others perhaps too quaint or ornate for today's taste, but all have a certain beauty and above all they are distinctive. The reason is not hard to find. The prince of each of these little states, despite his proud title, was a man with very little power. He could never recruit a large army and, whatever his nominal authority, his real ability to order the lives of his subjects was strictly limited. There had to be another outlet for his ambitions and he found it in architecture. In each state the princeling would engage an architect, from his own subjects if there was one good enough, if not from outside, and frequently the prince himself would contribute to the design. The materials would be found locally, local people did the work and the erection of an important new building was a major event in the state, something to be gazed at, criticised or admired but certainly not ignored. In Europe today it is still true that the smaller states have a higher concentration of the arts. For example, anyone visiting both Austria and Germany will be struck by the difference in their cultural endeavours. The large *länder* of modern Germany, where the little states and principalities have been merged together, are near to becoming cultural deserts; libraries, literary societies, theatres, opera houses, and art galleries are fewer, and people do show less interest in them. It is very different in Austria, yet the Austrians are just as German as anyone living in the Federal Republic.

Paradoxically, one reason why a small social unit can be more congenial to creativity is that it can provide a greater experience of diversity. When people, especially young people, migrate from Little Bumbleton to London they may be seeking the greater opportunities and the wider choice of lifestyles that the big city offers. The trouble is that when they get there most of them settle into a coterie of people similar to themselves. What the eighteen-year-old migrant to London actually looks for is a larger circle of late teenagers with the same tastes as his or her own. The same thing is true to people of all ages: we all tend to seek the company of people of our own kind. In a small community we are more or less obliged to confront people of types, classes, and lifestyles very different from our own, but in the big city we can easily restrict our circle to 'people like us'. What is true within communities is also true in the world at large. The existence of a large number of small, largely independent societies does not produce a parochial culture. Just the reverse. The interaction between differing societies, like the interaction between differing people, breaks down complacency and prevents stagnation. A good example is to be found in English classical architecture. This arose when the ideas and designs of the Italian Renaissance reached England and made its impact on the very different tradition of native architecture there. What came out of this cross-fertilisation was one of the great traditions of public and domestic building, and it grew up precisely because England and Italy had been developing separately and along different lines. In a homogenised Europe nothing of that sort could happen. Self-contained and uniform, it would truly be a parochial place, and if history is a guide, we would expect its contribution to the creative arts to be dismally low. Indeed, the homogenisation (an ugly word for an ugly process) has begun: what difference can we see between the office blocks, great slabs of glass and steel, going up in London, Paris, Berlin, and Madrid?

6

Europe Out of Control

The argument of this book so far has been a general one. Although there is no law that makes political units grow ever larger, there are strong forces pushing in that direction, not the least being the lust for power present in individual people and in certain groups. The people concerned are often those who feel frustrated in their own lives so, as cities and states grow larger and their citizens more powerless to control them, a vicious circle will emerge. The result of this social elephantiasis is an erosion of the civic bond which holds people together in communities that are on a human scale, and once that bond is weakened there is a corresponding breakdown of the civil order so crime and alienation spread through society. The economic enrichment that many people hope for from big states, big markets, and big corporations is at least in part illusory. The citizens of a small state can be just as prosperous and are often more so and they are also more likely to be culturally creative. The belief that federalism is necessary to prevent the wars that would inevitably break out between nation states is equally unfounded, harking back to an earlier and different stage in history.

The question now is how all this applies to Britain and Europe at the present critical time.

For a start it is easy to see how the love of power has, in the past, so often been the motive for bringing Europe under a single rule. From Julius Caesar and Charlemagne through to Napoleon and Hitler, no one need mistake the arrogance of conquest for a benign desire to bring order and peace. It is also not hard to see that same love of power in the handful of politicians, civil servants, diplomats, and mega-businessmen who will have control of the new European Union if it is ever successfully created. They may, like the conquerors, claim that theirs is a great civilising mission, but if they believe their own claim it merely shows how large is man's capacity for self-delusion.

Already Europe has come a long way in truncating the power of the nation states that compose the Union and in so doing it has produced a manifest 'democratic deficit'. That phrase comes not from some Euro-sceptic but from the European Parliament itself and there is no denying its truth. Democracy means that citizens should only be bound by laws to which they, or at least a majority of them, have consented. Every law, after all, takes away some freedom, for there is no point in a law unless it prevents people doing something they would otherwise have done or obliges them to do something they would not have chosen to do. In the same way every tax takes money away from someone who, left to himself, would have spent it differently. Of course it is right and necessary for every civilised society to impose the rule of law and to raise taxes, but a free and democratic state, where individual liberty is held in esteem as a political principle, does not do so without allowing its citizens to raise their voices and then acting on the consensus of their wishes.

The democratic deficit has arisen in Europe because the Union has taken powers away from the component states, which are subject to democratic control, and given it to centralised authorities which are not. Indeed we need to ask whether the countries in the European Union can still rightly be called nation states since they are no longer free to exercise the powers that define a nation state as such.

There are five of these critical powers, and any student of the Treaty of Rome must agree that all but one of them has been lost. The first is the power to make law, and Article 189 of the Treaty of Rome is drafted in plain enough terms. The Council of Ministers is made into a legislature and any regulation it passes becomes the law of the European Union. No ratifying procedure by elected representatives of the people is required. Measures with the force of law have issued from the Council in their thousands.

The second power, the power to tax, is also in the hands of the Council. There are rules governing the rates of VAT that member states impose. Also import levies and duties are an important form of revenue in the Community's budget and since many of them constitute a tax on food they have an inescapable impact on everyone, but particularly on the poor for whom food is a major part of family expenditure.

The third power is the power to interpret law. There is now a large body of Community law and, as a result of the Maastricht Treaty, the European Court of Justice has an increasing role in interpreting the law, along with the power to fine a national government if it fails to enforce that law. On many occasions British courts have had to refer decisions to the European Court and have been bound by its judgements.

As to the fourth power, the power to make treaties with other countries, negotiations for a treaty concerning trade with a country outside the Union are, by the Treaty of Rome, entirely a matter for the Commission – and the treaty itself is in the hands of the Council of Ministers without any need for ratification in the parliaments of member states. In the setting up of the World Trade Organisation to replace GATT, Britain had no part; the negotiations were by the European Commission and the new treaty was signed by a Commissioner on behalf of the European Union as a supranational power.

Only the power to declare war is still left exclusively in the hands of national governments and it is difficult to see how that could survive the creation of a common European defence policy, which the federalists are anxious to achieve.

Does it matter that these powers have been transferred? Are they not constitutional niceties of little concern to ordinary people? In the early days of the Community's development that may have been so; apart from the Common Agricultural Policy not much was administered in Brussels and the legislative and fiscal powers of coercion were invoked on such a modest scale that their impact on most people's lives was trivial. That cannot be said now.

As power accumulates in Brussels the democratic deficit grows greater and that becomes more and more obvious in the way in which new laws and taxes are introduced. Each one begins as a proposal by the Commission to the Council of Ministers and they have no direct mandate of authority from the people but only from their governments. The Council sits in secret behind closed doors and no member of the public nor representatives of the media attend so as to report how a decision has been reached. The regulations and directives cascade out of Brussels at a rate that shows no sign of slackening; indeed, with the Treaty of Maastricht, a whole new range of governmental functions passed to the European empire. They include monetary policy, with extended authority to control the economies of the member states, transport, environment, immigration, citizenship, education, and vocational training. Clearly these touch the lives of every sector of society in every corner of the Community. Although the press and the other media are not allowed to hear the discussions or to know how or why the ministers reach their decisions, we do know that a great deal of horse-trading goes on. Several proposals are usually submitted at the same time and, as the bargaining over them goes on, each minister gives priority to the ones that effect the most politically important interests in his country. In return he must be prepared to give way on other issues, however foolish he thinks the proposals are and even if they will be damaging to a minority. Anomalies and absurdities thus arise, and sometimes injustices. Even if they did not, the procedure can scarcely be consistent with any interpretation of democracy.

The arguments for this secrecy are exactly the same as were heard in England long ago, before the House of Commons admitted strangers to the gallery: debates held in private can be conducted with candour and without fear. We can see now that those arguments were mistaken and not many people would say that a return to secrecy in Parliament would be a step towards greater democracy or accountability.

The remedy, say the parliamentarians of Strasbourg, is to take legislative and fiscal powers from the Council of Ministers and have the Commission submit its proposals to the European Parliament, whose doors would be open to the public and the media. Three hundred and fifty million people would no longer be kept in ignorance of the reasons why they were to change their ways or pay new taxes.

This reform might make for greater openness, but real accountability is another matter. Once again the question of scale becomes all-important. Each MEP's constituency contains about half a million people. Any one voter therefore has a negligible say in who represents him, and even if the candidate he favours is elected he will, when he gets to Strasbourg, be only one among over five hundred. Large and vocal interest groups can hope to have their voices heard but ordinary men and women have little chance. If they are to have any influence at all they must depend on their Member finding some way of being sensitive to their needs.

With the best will in the world he will only be able to do so most imperfectly. My own constituency as a Member of the British Parliament gives me nearly sixty-five thousand people to represent in the House of Commons. By spending every weekend and every day of the parliamentary recesses meeting my constituents I might, in the course of a year, be able to talk to a thousand of them long enough to get beyond the particular problems they have brought to my 'surgery' and learn something of their deeper hopes and fears. In practice, of course, there are many other things to do and even the most conscientious MP can never hope to make significant contact with more than two or three hundred constituents a year.

There is also the question of what sort of people the MEP meets. If he visits a school it is not the junior teacher or the cleaner who will claim his attention, but the head or the chairman of governors. At the factory it will be the managing director not the lad crouched over a computer or a lathe. If he walks round a housing estate he will meet those who are at home, which automatically excludes the ordinary men and women out at work. And all the time an inner circle of people who are primarily responsible for organising the member's support in the constituency will inevitably have prior calls on him. The truth is that a district or county councillor can make real contact with a true cross-section of his electorate and a parish councillor can do so easily; a Member of Parliament cannot and for a member of the European Parliament it is doubly impossible.

There are, of course, a number of hopes and fear that are common, if not to everyone, at least to a large number of us – the hope for a good job and a pleasant home, the hope for a good education for one's children, the fear of becoming redundant at fifty and never finding another job, the mixed hopes and fears with which most people look forward to retirement. These feelings are obvious, widely shared and easily understood, but there are others that go deeper and may not be so readily articulated. What kind of country will our children and grandchildren live to see? Is it steadily in decline or can it somehow revive its fortunes? What sort of society are we creating when scarcely a house is safe from thieves? Will the tide of crime ever turn, and how do we tackle it? Must drug addiction go on spreading, and what can we do to save our children from it? Most of us are concerned with these things because we have feelings not just for ourselves but for the city, town, or village we live in, and for our country. In the 1950s and 1960s the party manifestos, political speeches, and newspaper comments reflected this. They were not nationalistic or chauvinist but patriotic in the true sense, in that they were about a love of country. This is a sentiment that nowadays is not always understood by politicians and never by the spin doctors, advertising agents, and public relations gurus who in the last two decades have been recruited by political parties to advise them on how to garner votes. It is hardly surprising that political advertising has sunk to pandering to the lowest of the electorate's materialistic instincts, for that is how the trade of these recruits has operated in other spheres.

One way and another, patriotism has had a bad press lately. Of course it can be perverted: at the extreme it can turn into the racism and aggression of the Nazis. But it is important to recognise that that is a perversion and we must not judge good impulses by their perverted forms. If we did, we should have to outlaw love because of rapists. The trouble with trying to outlaw patriotism is that what replaces it is not, except in a few idealistic people, a pure love of all humanity (or even all European humanity) but a concentration on narrow, selfish interest.

Because they are committed to a supranational Europe, the federalists are forced to downplay the patriotism still felt by people in nation states. They do so at their peril. In the end people's emotions are stronger than the imperatives of administrative convenience, and attempts to suppress them can have disastrous consequences. We noted earlier the counter-current described by John Naisbitt in which, as economic cosmopolitan-ism takes over, people with a linguistic or cultural identity start to demand political independence. This is one factor that is going to exert a strong centrifugal force in any over-centralised Europe. There are others, and between them they present a real threat that such a Europe would be so unstable that in the end it would break up. When large centralised federations fly apart the results are usually calamitous. History provides enough examples and before we commit ourselves to a course that may end in that way we should take a hard, clear look at the forces that could destroy a federal Europe.

One thing which has already roused a great deal of popular hostility is the sheer inefficiency of the European Union. The grotesquely high cost of frauds riding on the back of the Common Agricultural Policy has been mentioned, but even if there were no fraud at all the CAP would impose a heavy burden on every family in the European Union. In return, so far from protecting the countryside it has subsidised its destruction. People know this, and know that the only reason the tragi-comedy is allowed to continue is that there has been a political stitch-up between the ministers of the large continental countries. So far, agriculture and fishing are the only industries governed in detail by the European Union. If similar distortions were imposed on other industries by the expanding European the result could be disastrous, especially as competition grows ever hotter in the global market. Already rules and restrictions have reduced the competitiveness of European industry and Britain has been wise to opt out of some of them. As the effect of centralised interference becomes more and more evident, other countries are likely to demand a reduction in the scope of central power.

If inefficiency is the indirect result of any large-scale bureaucracy, the direct cost is also large. Abstract ideas about the 'economy of scale' are very misleading here. As the state grows in size so does the complexity of its problems. With the growth, the ratio of governors to governed has to change. In a homogeneous, self-governing village community the administration can be left in the hands of a single person doing whatever is necessary in his or her spare time. But as a community grows the work of administration increases, not in proportion to the rising population but exponentially. In a community of a hundred with just one person giving a few hours to the task of administration only 0.25 per cent of the people are engaged in it. Let the community explode to a million people and 5 per cent may join officialdom. Should it grow to a state the size of Britain or France 10 per cent may well become bureaucrats of one kind or another, which as a proportion is forty times as large as in the original community. By that time there will be a steady stream of new policies and programmes to regulate the many conflicts of interest among the population, and every social and economic problem will have become increasingly complex and intractable.

Now merge together into one union fifteen or more states with a population of over 350 million, with fourteen or fifteen different languages and cultures, and with so many conflicting interests that it would be impossible to list them all. The increase in the potential size of the bureaucracy is now beyond calculation. Of course the potential will never be reached, but the bureaucratic machine will for ever have a pretext to expand. As it is, hundreds of directives and regulations flow out of Brussels every year. Does anyone believe that there will ever come a day when the flow will dry up and officials in Brussels will announce that there is no longer any necessity for them to think up new laws for the rest of us to obey? By contrast, in a small state the size of Switzerland bureaucratic activity is static; indeed New Zealand has seen a considerable decline and the proportion of the gross domestic product spent by the government is due to fall to thirty-five per cent, compared to an expected rise in the European Union to fifty per cent.

Another source of possible conflict with the European Union lies in the disparities between different countries and regions in Europe. One of the reasons for regional hostility within states is a sense by one region that it is being held back or held down by another. So the Scots believe the English in the south-east are prospering at their expense, the Flemings believe the same about the Walloons and the Catalans about the Andalusians, while the Germans on the Rhine grow ever more anxious about the cost of absorbing Brandenburg. Feelings of envy and even hate arise and they will be exacerbated by economic recession. If the economy of the European Union persists in being in competition with the burgeoning industries of Asia the days when its people could expect an ever-rising standard of living may be over. What is more, if a very high level of unemployment continues – more than, say, ten per cent – social and political dangers will be added to the political ones. These will make it imperative for more regional aid to be given to the areas of the highest unemployment, and although this may be socially and politically wise, such large-scale subsidies will have to be paid for by the more prosperous parts of the Union. The consequent taxation will weaken the stronger elements of the economy; taxing competitive industries in order to subsidise uncompetitive ones is a prescription for economic decline and it ends not in relieving unemployment but in making it worse.

The scale of this problem will grow enormously if the states of Eastern Europe are admitted to the European Union, though in the end it seems likely that they will have to be, and indeed the Union can hardly claim to be 'Europe' if they are not. The challenge is to end the division of Europe that has brought so much misery to so many millions of people; and for us in the West to sit back on the pretext that we have our own problems and we are loath to share our lot with the East would be truly anti-European. Yet the difficulties of unifying East with West Germany will have been a mere foretaste of the spate of problems that will arise from trying to incorporate the old Iron Curtain countries into the present Union of Western Europe.

Any attempt to bring those countries up to the level of the West will involve huge transfers of capital and that will just be the start of it. On top of all the economic difficulties there will be severe political problems as well. In Russia, Ukraine, Bulgaria, and Slovakia it is difficult to perceive an instinct for robust democracy, and if their fragile political and economic systems collapse the rubble could spill into Poland, Hungary, and the Czech Republic. Perhaps the one-time Communist states will muddle through and at least a semblance of democracy will survive, but what will they feel about joining a European Union whose capital is far away in Brussels and whose constitution will take away so much of the freedom they have struggled to gain, and whose help in their crisis was so dismal? The people of Moscow, St. Petersburg, and Kiev can hardly be expected to hurry very fast to Brussels; the brave people of Warsaw have no particular reason to trust those to the east or the west of them and, having fought so valiantly for their independence and the right to govern themselves they may show a little reluctance to hand it over so soon.

A further intractable problem for any European Union of the future will be the disparity in power that comes from disparity in economic performance. One of the prime arguments for political union was that it would eliminate the risk of war, particularly another war between France and Germany, and although we have seen that to be unnecessary it was an acknowledgment that German power presented a threat. For a century Germany tried to impose her dominance by military means: now she is able to do so by economic means. She is unquestionably the dominant industrial power in Europe and she is not going to agree to any developments that threaten her wealth or reduce her ability to follow her own course. Why should she be told where to go by less successful nations? To believe that Germany will become 'Europeanised' in the sense that she will surrender her own national interests to appease the other states of the Union, and that she will allow them to go on indefinitely feeding off the billions of deutschmarks that she provides with no apparent advantage in exchange – that is to dream of a new and very implausible theory of international relations.

It is instructive, though sad, to see how in Germany wealth and industrial power have not eliminated distrust and even hatred of foreigners. Immigrants are treated with brutality and neo-Nazis are on parade. They are, of course, a small minority but they show to an extreme degree what many ordinary people feel in a more moderate way; a wish to live in a nation that is a recognizable entity. In the end it is this that will become the focus for the discontent with 'Europe' that will be the inevitable effect of trying to produce homogeneity in such a heterogeneous collection of states.

"Having made Italy, we must now make Italians," said Miasma Taparelli d'Azeglio when a unified Italy was born. That was in 1861, and in all the intervening years that aim has not been achieved. A majority in Lombardy now wants to sever links not just with Sicily but with all the southern half of Italy, and Italy is probably less unified today than at any period in this century. She is not alone in this difficulty. As Umberto Bossi raises the cry of "*secessione*" in the foothills of the Italian Alps, on the other side of the mountains the politicians in Munich demand more responsibilities for the *länder*, and when the centre of Germany's power moves from Bonn to Berlin the Bavarians are joined by others. A united nation has prompted many questions for the German people: will they be impoverished by the East, and if so ought not the *länder* to have more control over public expenditure? Will the much-enlarged Germany not make the government too remote and insensitive to the needs of the periphery?

The three other large member states of the European Union are experiencing similar strains. In Spain both the Catalans and the Basques are fervent in their demands for greater autonomy, and in France the voice of the Bretons is raised more loudly than ever. Of course every self-respecting Frenchman outside Paris has always had a disdain for what might be decreed in the capital, but the murmuring for constitutional change can now be heard quite distinctly. In Britain the very name 'United Kingdom' is coming to seem more and more like a misnomer as nationalism in Scotland and Wales gains ground and is no longer regarded as an aberration but as a permanent force that must be reckoned with, while in Northern Ireland the third option of Ulster independence is canvassed by one of the three major parties.

These regional discontents are part fuelled by the sense referred to earlier, that one's own region is being held back economically by others, but there is more to it than that. In the end it is human emotions that dominate politics. The architects of the Maastricht Treaty might echo d'Azecho and say, "Having made the European Union, we must now make Europeans," but that is an unreal ambition, never to be fulfilled. The treaty authorises a Committee of the Regions to be set up so that Catalans, Scots, Bretons, Bavarians, Sicilians, and many others can have a platform to voice their concerns independently of the national governments. Regions could form alliances across national frontiers with, for example, the Welsh, Bretons, and other Celts standing shoulder to shoulder against the wishes of London and Paris. Ultimately the federalists might hope that the middle ground would wash away and we would be left with a single European state with the region as the next smaller political unit. A man would think of himself as a European first and Scottish next, but no longer as British.

This might be a sensible idea but it would only work on the condition that the European central authority dramatically limited its own powers, to act as a mediator between the region-states and to deal only with those matters that they could not deal with separately. The principle of subsidiarity mooted at Maastricht is now seen as a dead duck. The only restraint on the central power would come from regional units, each of which was tiny compared with the Union itself, but once there is a single currency and the formality of economic and monetary union, the central power will be overwhelming. If Britain could not halt this process, Wales certainly could not. Without some much firmer and more permanent restraint on centralisation we should end up with a huge European super-state with few limits on the powers it could award itself and a greatly increased 'democratic deficit'. In the end, the hope that people would be held together by the civil bond of feeling themselves to be Europeans would prove vain.

The truth is that most people do not show any great enthusiasm for the 'European ideal'. Decades have gone by, there has been a huge propaganda effort financed by many millions of pounds of interested money and backed by governments and political parties. Still, when electorates have been consulted in referendums and opinion polls, only a marginal majority has been in favour of going along the present course. Further, one has to ask whether there would be a majority at all if people had been honestly told at the outset what was proposed. The founders of the EEC, we know now, had political objectives but they were never advertised. The goal was to be economic: merge the economies of the Six together and they would all grow prosperous. When Britain came to join, her people were assured that there would be no less of sovereignty, and even now we are being told that we are not be asked to give up our sovereignty only to 'pool' it – as if having the right to interfere in other people's affairs compensated us for giving them the right to interfere in ours.

People may tolerate incursions on their political independence if they feel that as a result they are materially better off, but we must not deceive ourselves into supposing that they are happy about it and are coming to think of themselves as real Europeans with a strong sense of loyalty to Europe as such. What will happen if the dream fades, the new industrial countries overtake us and we are faced with the brutal facts of economic decline? After Maastricht, the Union can scarcely be allowed by the Commission to slip back to being just a community, still less a customs union. To reassure the people of Western Europe that a rich future still lies ahead, a grand plan will have to be devised and Union-wide policies introduced to ensure 'growth', 'competitiveness', and any other ingredient of prosperity that the Commission and Council of Ministers may conceive. Unfortunately no such policies can be carried out without spending money and enforcing regulations – in short, without additional taxation and coercion. This might be acceptable if the new accretion of power could be devolved to the regions so that people could feel that the burdens they were being asked to bear were for their own benefit but this would be a denial by Brussels of its purpose in devising plans that were Union-wide. Without it, however, there would be an inevitable strengthening of the jealousy and fear between regions that we have already noted, and also between the states themselves.

The danger that lies ahead for the European Union, then, is the same as the danger confronting a company that has issued a false prospectus. At the outset the citizens of countries joining the Common Market were assured that it would make them richer without encroaching on their political independence. As more and more power has been handed over to the European authorities there have been strenuous efforts to persuade us all that the development of a superstate is beneficial and, in any case, inevitable. It has been the aim of this book to show that it is neither, but rather that it will reduce people's real welfare and satisfaction because of the fundamental inferiority of very large social and political units. So far there has been fairly steady economic growth in Europe, as there has throughout the industrialised world, but now the competition is hotting-up; relative to the Asian countries we are already in decline and the time may come when we find ourselves in absolute decline, our standard of living no longer rising but steadily falling. If that happens the internal tensions in Europe, between regions and between states, will become more and more evident, with the more successful demanding to be freed from the hampering weight of the more backward, and the latter becoming increasingly envious of the former.

Inevitably there will be strong and perhaps irresistible demands for autonomy, for escape from the huge, cumbersome, top-heavy edifice that is now being constructed. The greatest danger is that, by the time this happens, the coherence and authority of the European member-states will have been eroded and largely dismantled so that we will not easily be able to return to where we were before. The nature of what we are now creating will then become plain even to the most myopic; and it will not prove to be a community of Europeans, only a continent full of stateless persons.

7

Another Europe for the Electronic Age

Monnet, Schuman, Spinelli, and other architects of 'an ever-closer union' knew nothing of e-mail, the fax, the superhighway, or even the first generation of computers. They were not to know how our world would change with the wonders of telecommunications. Their successors in the 1990s have no such excuse. They have to face the fact that one of the reasons why the European super-state is obsolete before its structure has been completed is that the whole business of making decisions and putting them into effect can now be something totally different from what it was before. Let us now look at how it can change the way we are governed. As there is a difference between 'can' and 'will' we should then consider why this potential change will be made; it will not come about because the existing decision-makers, the governors, will surrender their powers by their own volition, but because the governed will no longer tolerate their sense of powerlessness.

This new technology has done more to break down the barriers in international trade than all the many GATT negotiations put together: without it the global economy, far from being a fact, would be no more than an empty phrase.

In his *Global Paradox* John Naisbitt has explained how the telecommunications revolution will burst out in four different ways. First is the hybridisation of computers, telephones, and television. Each of these three is acquiring the abilities of the others. By themselves they are means of communication, each valuable in itself, but once fused together they become an instrument of power as well. In the hands of the ordinary individual – the private citizen, as distinct from the employee in a business enterprise – this multi-purpose piece of equipment will empower him to spread his views and sentiments to an audience that no conventional public meeting could match.

Secondly there are the global alliances now being created embryonically. Once a common interest is found, an alliance to pursue a common aim follows naturally. Until today, the ability to find others with the same interest has been limited to people one could communicate with by conventional means. Telephoning a hundred other people can take a long time; writing them letters can take longer. An advertisement in a local newspaper may reach more than a hundred, but the business of getting them together to decide upon a common aim and how it is to be achieved may take many days of effort. The end result will be puny compared with what will be achieved when the communication can stretch round the globe and answers are computerised into conclusions within a few seconds. One individual sitting by himself in a mountain cabin miles away from the rest of the human race will have the capability to start rolling all manner of new ideas, if not a revolution. The hustings revived with a vengeance! One can envisage numerous new alliances being established; and if the common interest crosses international frontiers, the alliances themselves will be transnational and all the more powerful for being so. Moreover, these alliances on single or limited issues will create a challenge to the democratic process in its present form. Will politicians and civil servants be able to adapt to the change? Can we picture the scene in Brussels in the year 2015? Hundreds and hundreds of pan-European alliances have got together, by then, and every minute of the day and night they bombard the Berlaymont, demanding answers, action information, consultation, and yet another meeting. What price, then, Big Government?

The third feature of the revolution is how the information superhighway will develop. Naisbitt believes the term is misleading, for it suggests something planned and thus imposed from above. Instead, he believes it comes from below, from the lowest level of the pyramid of human society – from ordinary people with extraordinary technology.

There will not just be a network of telecommunications, but a network of networks. A network of, let us say, geneticists working in commercial laboratories is formed. There is also a network of Roman Catholic priests, and one of scientific journalists, and one of academic ethicists. Then some discovery is made in one of the laboratories that may lead to a change in how we may view human life. Out it goes on one network after another, the criss-crossing of evidence and opinion begins, and so it goes beyond those four networks to anyone who wishes to take part in the debate. The whole world, quite literally, can have its tuppence worth. No longer need Mr and Mrs

64

Ordinary just sit at home muttering about the state of the world, unable to do anything themselves to put it right.

In this myriad of networks interflowing and interacting around the globe, every scintilla of human wisdom can find a niche. If it conjures up a latter-day Tower of Babel, it also ensures an interchange of views among different cultures, educations, and philosophies. Prejudices and preconceptions should at least be modified, and several degrees of understanding should be secured. Universal unanimity will be beyond hope – and probably undesirable anyway – but groups of networks as well as individual networks may reach a consensus good enough for changes of policy and a new programme of action.

The fourth element in the revolution is the personal telecomputer available for everyone. The telecomputer is the marvel that will transmit, receive and store information by voice, data-image, and video. It is going to be so small that it can sit in the palm of a hand and fit into a pocket or the corner of a handbag. As we walk along the street or travel in the train, mow the lawn, or play with the children, an immense mass of information will be there alongside us – and we will be able to pass it on (time permitting) to the rest of the human race. As these telecomputers become smaller and cheaper, so they will spread; and if not everyone in Outer Mongolia is yet quite computer-literate, it will soon be apparent to them all that these little marvels are worth a purchase.

Still more electronic marvels are to come. Digital technology will enable most of the world's working population to do their job anywhere, no matter how remote a corner they choose, and this is bound to begin a migration of countless millions on a scale never know before. It is our natural instinct to live with our own kind – our kindred spirits – and they are, we have to admit, not necessarily our relations, neighbours, or fellow employees. Networking around the globe, we will find many others with a similar outlook and interests. Why not get closer to them? Not even the uttermost wonders of telecommunications can be a substitute for living among those with whom we have so much in common. To imagine that one day a telecomputer will simulate a handshake or a pat on the back is a little too fanciful. Even smiles and laughter shared on the telecomputer can never be quite the same as they are at first-hand. So we can envisage new communities being created, a few hundred or thousands perhaps, but also some where much larger numbers come together to share the same values and beliefs.

To a greater extent than ever before, people will be able to choose which country to live in, and they will naturally be drawn to the one that best matches their own personality. For example, in Ireland the climate is mild and it rains a lot; the people are easy-going and hospitable, and do not take life too seriously; there is beautiful countryside and not much in the way of international culture. Even that modest description, if it is accurate, is enough to let anyone decide whether they would be content to live there. Now if another million or two migrated to Ireland because they relished its Irishness and a million or two left to go where they felt they would be more at home (ski-ing in the Alps, perhaps, or going to the opera house once a fortnight, or even imbibing the work ethic of the Rhine) the paradoxical consequence would be that Ireland would become more Irish than ever and its people more different from others in the European Union.

The same process is likely to take place in any region that has distinctive features with an obvious appeal to many who do not live there now. Scotland, Brittany, Bavaria, Tuscany, and Provence are examples, and as the new technology allows people to live and work in them who could never have done so in the past, so their human and social characteristics will become accentuated.

How many millions of Europeans will take advantage of this new freedom to move must be left to the imagination, although two other factors will play a part. Whilst travel has been considerably easier within the Continent and families and friends of one's youth can still be visited many times more easily than a few decades ago, we cannot be sure of the future cost of travel. For environmental reasons, if no other, it is probably going to rise quite steeply. The other factor is language, still a major barrier to migration within the Community. It is true that English is the second language in every European country and that this makes it easier for a Finn to speak to his new neighbours in Portugal, but there can be no true assimilation unless the language of one's adopted country becomes one's own.

Monnet, Schuman, Spinelli, and the other founding fathers would have applauded a mass-migration; the interflow of millions across ancient frontiers would be, to them, a sure sign that the people of Europe were thirsting to be true Europeans. In reality the very opposite is almost certain to be the case. As people sort themselves out into communities and countries according to their own natures and preferences, those countries will acquire more strongly individual characteristics. So far from becoming uniformly European, they will become more different, and they will guard their right to be different all the more jealously.

Overwhelmingly, the people of Europe, wherever they live, will wish to be on friendly terms with their fellow Europeans and will agree that trading together is as good a way as any other to cement friendly relationships. But such genial sentiments are nothing to do with sharing a common system of government, and the greater the diversity the more difficult and inappropriate it becomes to impose uniform laws, regulations, and taxes.

For most of us this freedom to move to a particular region or even an area within a region will be very desirable; being able to choose to live in one of perhaps hundreds of different localities because it happens to suit us better than any of the others is indeed a freedom worth having. But it will bring with it a dangerous side-effect that must be faced and guarded against. This is the development of new areas inhabited only by those who cannot escape from them. Would not most people prefer to live in Tuscany rather than Tyneside; Devonshire rather than Dusseldorf? Putting it bluntly, who on earth would want to go on living in Slough or Luton if they could do the same job with the same income in the Côte d'Azur or at least in one of England's more attractive corners? People with jobs that can be performed electronically will move to where they find it congenial; people without such jobs will have to stay behind and areas that already have an air of depression, such as some of the inner cities, will become more depressed. They then will begin to sink in a downward spiral. The more they look depressed, the more those who can leave will do so. As the houses empty, so property prices fall, and people move into the area, not out of choice, but for the worst of all reasons. The downward spiral continues its awful fall until the area becomes a physical mess of crime, discontent, misery, and alienation fit only for a Dickensian pen to describe. Anyone who has spent any time in certain parts of Liverpool, Manchester, or Birmingham will not hesitate to question the scenario, for it is beginning to happen already not just in those three inner cities, but in nearly all the old manufacturing centres of Britain as well as in several on the Continent. One or two exceptions can be named, like Glasgow; but that once great city has gained a new life only with the aid of many millions of pounds of subsidies from both London and Brussels, equivalent to thousands of pounds per head of the population. The cost of repeating the operation in all the cities and areas degraded by migration in the future would be beyond reckoning. Would the other regions be willing to be taxed the necessary proportion of their income? The envy and resentment that already exist between poor and rich regions would be greatly aggravated, and nothing could be more calculated to dash the quest for pan-European unity.

For yet another reason, the new technology is going to thwart the centralisation of power. Already a conference of a few people, each thousands of miles from any of the others, can take place telephonically, and we are approaching the time when a large number of persons, even hundreds, will be able to take part in a conference conducted in as orderly and effective a way as one held in conventional circumstances. Whether the conference is of politicians, business leaders or academics, whether national or international, the digital technology thus harnessed opens an enormous potential for good or ill. Telecommunications, having diffused power to everyone who possesses a telecomputer, now goes further and concentrates power in the hands of the owners who form themselves into some sort of organisation, while remaining far apart from one another. What would Robespierre or Lenin have given for such power; how much sooner and more easily would their revolutions have broken out?

Before the electronic age, a dissident had a hard task to bring together others of like mind. Surreptitious meetings at street corners or in nondescript cafes, printing leaflets and furtively handing them around – the pettiness and tedium of such means have deterred many from a new crusade. How different it will be in the future when one person, never leaving home, will be able to establish a network of fellow crusaders, and then, with everyone still staying at home, hold huge conferences to attract the media, which in turn multiplies the message. In the context of the European Community this diffusion of power will give minorities a political strength that hitherto has been denied them. Moreover, minorities will have the means of linking up together to forge coalitions as often as they may wish, holding mass conferences daily if necessary, instead of annually now. Walloons, Bretons, Basques, Bavarians, Welsh, Corsicans, and many other minorities will have a technology to secure their aims, which will probably be more effective than any campaign of violence or civil disobedience. It brings up-to-date the old adage about the pen being mightier than the sword. The sword is of the moment, the fear is momentary; but the pen records words that may never perish, and that makes it all the more dangerous. As the computer takes over the role of the pen, being able to store away vast amounts of beliefs and opinions as well as facts, it is going to be no friend to any authoritarian regime. So long as just one owner of a telecomputer with a record of liberty's story is still living in some remote corner of the globe, the world's dictators will never be safe. Telecommunications, far from making men and women slaves of technology as once was feared, will be on the side of the individual against the state, supporting the minority against the mega-state. Everyone willing to master the new techniques becomes empowered to an extent no ordinary person has ever been in the past.

Will this empowerment be for a new elite, limited to those who have acquired mastery over this instrument of power? Such a denial of the democratic process would certainly provoke a reaction by the underclass of computer-illiterates. However, Bill Gates, the genius of Microsoft, is as optimistic about this aspect of the revolution, in which he has played such a notable part, as he is about the rest of the scenario he forecasts. Once the technology is used to formulate or assess public opinion it can be made available in public libraries, civic offices, and official agencies with qualified staff in attendance to assist anyone disabled by poverty, illiteracy, or other handicaps. In his book *The Road Ahead*, Gates predicts that in less than twenty years time – by the year 2015 – we could all be equal in the use of the marvels of the electronic age. No-one seems to have questioned his estimate.

All this will have an incalculable impact on the world of politics, in which the telecomputer is going to replace much of the present mechanism of decision-making. Some futurists go so far as to foresee all of it replaced and thus the end of the politician! The telecomputer of the future will be able to receive, store, and catalogue all the information that is made available to the government and the legislators. The ordinary member of the public will be in a position – if he or she wishes – to know and understand as much about a subject as the legislators themselves. The argument for a representative form of democracy now becomes decidedly fragile. We elect our member of parliament to make decisions about what we are to have and how we are to behave because we ourselves have neither the time nor the information to do so adequately, and because the business of debating the subject can be done more effectively by our elected representatives gathering together for the purpose. Digital technology will enable even a large electorate to conduct such a debate with each participant sitting at home. Electronic voting is already a practicality, and it will not be long before it can be adapted as a form of direct democracy. If millions feel powerless today, believing that they have little opportunity to participate in a democratic process, their feelings will change as soon as telecommunication is able to open the door. They will insist upon using their telecomputers to decide for themselves in a truly democratic way what laws are to be made for them to obey and what taxation is needed for their government. Clearly, the smaller and more homogeneous the state they live in, the more effective this kind of democracy will be.

To sum up, the information revolution will have two powerful effects that must be taken into account in designing any future political system, and in particular in setting a future pattern for Europe. First, it will encourage a new form of mobility that will stimulate the emergence of a large number of regions and communities each with a distinctive character of its own and a strong disinclination to be merged with other regions of a different character. Second, it will put in the hands of ordinary people a powerful mechanism for gathering information, conferring with others, reaching decisions, and communicating their wishes to the centres of decision-making.

One only has to state these effects to see how they run counter to the ideas of European federalists. Their concept is of a Europe that, in all the important respects that affect public policy, can be treated as homogeneous and can be ruled by a central elite, whether that elite consists of the Commission, the Council of Ministers, the European Parliament, or any other body that may be devised. Before we allow ourselves to be dragged any further down a European road whose direction was set by the idealists of the 1950s, almost half a century ago, we should rub our eyes, wake up, and recognise what kind of a world we are really going to be living in a few years from now.

8

As if People Mattered

Justice, wrote Aristotle, is not necessary among friends. Unfortunately we do not live only among friends, and in our present complex society, with its immense number of different occupations, recreations, values and ages, there are inevitable conflicts of interest. The task of civil decision-making cannot escape being contentious. How are all the conflicts to be reconciled, at every level from the personal to the international?

One solution, which in one form or another is common, is to have a multi-tiered government, with parishes that are autonomous in matters that affect their interests alone, then an intermediate tier of local government for districts or counties, and a national government at the head. However, we cannot stop there. There are conflicts of interest between states as there are between people and many attempts have been made to find a structure that will allow them to be peacefully resolved. Essentially these structures can take two forms; they can be international or supranational.

The international structure (some prefer to call it inter-governmental) leaves sovereignty with the nations, who retain the two centrally important powers of making laws and raising taxes. If they are unjust or oppressive they have only themselves to blame. There are numerous examples of such international bodies – the United Nations, the North Atlantic Treaty Organisation, the Council of Europe, and many others. Their effectiveness depends on the backing they get from their member states, and it fails unless the peoples of those states, through their elected governments, will them to succeed. In practice they have generally been successful, precisely because the arrangements have been freely entered into and the international body cannot impose its own policies on unwilling members.

By contrast, a supranational structure to some degree takes over the powers of law-making and taxation, and to the extent that it does, the member states lose their own sovereignty. This unquestionably is the structure of the European Union. The Treaty of Rome transferred the power to make laws from the national parliaments to the Council of Ministers; these laws cannot be amended or repealed by the national parliaments and they override any legislation already passed by those parliaments. Any new legislation must conform to whatever the Council of Ministers has agreed. The Council also has overriding powers of taxation that can be exercised over import duties, levies and, increasingly, value added tax. The Single European Act and the Treaty of Maastricht have taken the process of supranationalism several steps further and if a new federal union has not yet been born, that undoubtedly is the aim. Before we are irrevocably committed to it we should take the time to look at the fate of such federations, past and present, and to ask what are the conditions that make for their success or failure.

Most federal unions are doomed. Two notable examples in Europe have recently collapsed – the Soviet Union and Yugoslavia. The Central African Federation and the West Indian Federation lasted only a few years and very few federal unions have survived for more than half a century. Even some of those that have are beginning to look unstable: no-one predicts with certainty that Quebec will remain part of Canada, for example. It is worth considering what it is that makes for stability.

Two good examples are Germany and Australia and the key there is that culturally and linguistically they are single nations. Bavarians and Prussians may deny that they are alike and certainly there are tensions between the *länder*, but at root both are Germans. With regard to Australia, what outsider could tell the difference between anyone from Perth and Sydney? Homogeneity is the key to success, a broad similarity of values and interests, while the sharing of a language creates a common culture and a means of understanding.

The United States has endured as a federal union for two centuries, though after less than one century its unity was tested by an internal war known, depending on your viewpoint, as the civil war or the war between the states. In its early years the USA also had cultural and linguistic homogeneity, and though that is no longer so, the union is held together by a system of checks and balances built into the constitution. Some of the most important of these deal with the problem of imbalance between the individual states. It is generally true that for a federation to be successful its constituent states or

72

nations must be of roughly equal size and power. Clearly that is not true in the USA; there is no comparison between Texas and Rhode Island, for example. Nevertheless, both those states have exactly the same legislative and fiscal powers, as do all the others, and each sends just two senators to represent it at the federal level. Under the American constitution no state can acquire hegemony over another.

Other constitutional checks limit the powers of the President and the federal government generally. The relationships are nicely balanced between the President and the state governors, and also between the Senate and House of Representatives in Washington and their counterparts in the states. Watching over them all is the guardian of the constitution, the Supreme Court.

It is true that federal powers have increased considerably since the days of President Roosevelt, largely as a result of the power to raise and spend revenue, but even so, the states retain far-reaching powers that in many ways are greater than those of the member states of the European Union. Furthermore, and most importantly, any attempt to transfer more powers from the states to Washington would mean amending the constitution, and that would be decisively resisted.

Contrast all this careful system of checks and balances with the situation in the European Union. The most glaringly obvious difference is that Europe has no constitution. In America a group of wise men (and they were wise) set down at the outset the precise details of the political structure they were creating. In Europe, nothing of the sort happened, and for a very good reason. The politicians who planned the eventual federation of Europe knew that if they put that plan to their electorates there would be an overwhelming vote of "No" in every one of their countries. As a result there is no limit set on the powers that may be transferred to Brussels. Everything is up for negotiation and that will mean what it always means: the drift of power to the centre will continue. Also, since the countries of Europe are even more disparate in size and wealth than the states of America and since no proper system of balance between them has been set up, in the end the most powerful will get their way.

If the United States is a good example for Europe, Switzerland is a better one. Her critics may complain that she is rather too clinical in everyday life and her people too self-disciplined for comfort, but what cannot be denied is that her federal system has survived for five centuries while all around her other countries disintegrated in wars and revolution. Half a millennium! Here we have a small country whose five and a half million people are divided up into twenty-two cantons each of which enjoys a large measure of self-government. On the whole, the cantons have more autonomy than the individual states of the USA, and more than Britain will enjoy if the Maastricht Treaty comes fully into effect. Within the frontiers of Switzerland, Germans, French, Italians, and a small number of Romansch have lived in peace for many generations, at times when their cousins over the border have been steeped in hatred of one another, eager to slaughter and be slaughtered. It is an amazing record and there is only one rational explanation of how this harmony has been achieved. The key lies in the very smallness of the cantons and in the fact that none can have the power to dominate or overrule any of the others, each being of much the same size and strength as its neighbours.

The contrast with the European Union is stark. Of the fifteen member states of the Union, five are considerably larger than the other ten, while one of the five – Germany – is itself a federal union, and is unquestionably stronger than the other four, so strong, indeed, that it is difficult to think of any occasion when its interests have not prevailed over the others. In a union of that sort strength is power, unless that strength is bridled by constitutional mechanisms; and it is hardly necessary to point out that Germany has not so far agreed to be subjected to the same kind of checks that operate between the states of the USA.

A few years ago the *Wall Street Journal* said that it should not be Switzerland joining the European Community but *vice versa*. It meant that the architects of the Community should model their dream on a Switzerland writ large, and there would then be a realistic prospect of harmony among the member states. At the very least there is a great deal to be learnt from the success of the Swiss experiment, and it is worth taking a look at its history. It can afford to be brief, for Switzerland illustrates the old adage about happy countries having little history.

It was not until Napoleon invaded Switzerland and established what was to be called the Helvetic Republic that the country was truly integrated into a state. Before that the cantons had been largely autonomous and no doubt geography played a part in dividing the communities from each other. They first came together into a loose confederation in 1291 when the 'Federal Letter' was written, under which three of the cantons pledged support to the others against the threat of the Hapsburgs. One by one the other cantons joined in and the Swiss Confederation was born. Its purpose was self-defence and it remained so throughout its existence, leaving all the other functions of government with the cantons. Since their total populations never exceeded a million, government stayed very close to the governed. As in the rest of Europe, women were excluded from the franchise, but about half the men had full civic rights, a higher proportion than anywhere else on the Continent.

The American Revolution had a major effect upon the Swiss. The Declaration of Independence and the foundation of a new federal union led the peoples of Switzerland to wonder whether they were slipping behind in what today we would simply call democracy, but in those days was spoken of as the rights of the individual. As they debated the issue, Napoleon stepped in with his soldiers; the Swiss were now ready for change and Bonaparte gave it to them. Like all his plans, his proposals were neat and orderly: an integrated state with executive, legislature, and judiciary separated as Montesquieu would wish. But, as on most occasions, he went too far. The notion of an integrated state appealed to a minority, who saw the levers of power within their grasp, but the majority perceived the danger. In the diffusion of power rests the freedom to think and behave as we would wish, and the power to curb that freedom is only needed to prevent it being used to injure others. This principle, say many Swiss people, has given them their peace for hundreds of years, and it is not to be discarded without the most careful consideration of the consequences. The debate prevented a final conclusion, and with Napoleon's defeat the Congress of Vienna re-drew the maps of Europe. Switzerland, it was decided, should revert to what she was in 1797, the old Swiss Confederation.

This was not quite good enough for the Swiss, however. Philadelphia and Washington might be far away, but what had been said over there had found an echo in Berne and Zurich. Moreover, the liberal movement nearer home, not least in England, had its influence too. The outcome was the Swiss Federal Constitution of 1848 and, although substantially amended in 1874, it remains today. It is a compromise between a confederal system of cantonal independence and a centralised government. Advocates of the latter urged that a single trading area required a unified national state, with arguments not unlike those we have heard a century later in the European Community. The arguments, however, were rejected, and a hundred years have gone by to show them to have been fallacious. Under the constitution, defence and foreign affairs were to be the province of the federal state, as they were in the United States of America, but the autonomy of the canton in fiscal and economic matters was preserved.

Beneath the cantons are the *communes*. These carry out the functions of local government and, although some are no larger than an English parish, their responsibilities are comparable to those of both a county and district council in England. Decisions are made by the *commune* assembly, consisting of elected representatives, but in the smaller communes everyone can attend, speak, and vote. For a few thousand people to have their own unit of local government runs counter to the accepted wisdom in the rest of Western

Europe. We hear the cry from Whitehall, "it cannot be viable." That last word gets sorely abused. It is about what can live; and those who glibly speak of viability forget that small creatures are more lively than bigger ones. If a problem is on one's own doorstep, one is going to be more alive to it than if it were several miles away on someone else's doorstep. In the *commune's* assembly everyone has an interest in and a knowledge of what is on the agenda. Money is not spent unless they believe it is necessary expenditure that will have public approval and they can themselves witness how it is spent (it is their own money and money they themselves must raise from their neighbours). This makes for obvious economy, but the greatest saving is on administration, which, as we have noted, increases disproportionately as the unit of administration grows in size.

One would think that the efficiency, success, and longevity of the Swiss system would have persuaded the builders of the European Union at the least to take it seriously as a model. But no, all they see is the smallness of Switzerland and in their eyes smallness is contemptible. Kohl, Delors, Heath, and those lesser mortals who beaver away in Brussels have nothing but disdain for a vision of Europe based on little Switzerland, and those who glory in strength and admire bigness in all things will curl up their lips at a mere hint that she might have lessons for the rest of us to learn.

There is some hope, however, that this view will not pass unchallenged. Many officials of the Commission in Brussels have been eager to set up the Committee of the Regions under the Maastricht Treaty and they wish to see its consultative status transformed in due course to one with legislative and fiscal powers. As was noted in Chapter 6 this could be an excellent idea, but only if the European Union authorities restricted their own powers, as the Swiss federal government does, holding them within constitutional limits that could not be made to drift gradually outwards under pressure from the centralisers and the lovers of size.

If the creation of regional governments did happen, we should see the United Kingdom split into four, with France, Germany and the other large states similarly divided – there might be as many as a hundred 'regional states' in Europe. It would be important to ensure that none of them were so much larger or more powerful than the others that it could attempt to impose will on any of the others. Here as always it would be true that it is an imbalance of power that threatens conflict, as the strong see the opportunity to extort what they want from the weak.

If the European Union could be transformed into a scaled-up version of Switzerland in this way it would give it a real hope – perhaps the only hope – of surviving for more than a decade or two. However there is a formidable barrier to climb over before it can happen: France, Britain, Italy, and Spain, each of which has enough muscle in the councils of the European Union to obtain an advantage over the smaller members, would know that their power would be destroyed, while Germany's role as the dominant partner would immediately come to an end. It would demand real understanding and enlightenment on the part of their rulers to acknowledge that this might be in the interests of the people, not just in the small states but in the big ones too.

It may be that in the end Europe will learn from the example of others, for there is evidence of a widespread movement towards the dismantling of over-large political units. The growth in the number of nation states (up from 51 to 186 since the United Nations was founded after the Second World War) points strongly in that direction, and some futurists predict as many as a thousand by the middle of the twenty-first century. To assert, as some people do, that such small entities could not really be called nation states is to miss the point. Liechtenstein is truly a nation state, possessing all the powers that define one, and even with a thousand states the average population of each would still be something like 350,000, about fifteen times the size of Liechtenstein.

Even in the USA, despite the entrenched powers of the states, there are rumblings. In California, the State Assembly instituted a referendum on whether the state should be divided into three, and although the proposal was defeated, an overwhelming majority in northern California voted for the division. Throughout the USA, states' rights, the issue that brought about the Civil War is, after more than a century, once more a major subject of debate.

Such indicators give the lie to those who would like us to believe that maintaining and even increasing the independence of small nations is a retrograde, reactionary step. The truth is the reverse of that. We stand now at one of those points in history when the real change that is coming is a change in the direction of change. Progress no longer means bigger units of every kind. It means discriminating between those functions that are best carried out on a large scale and those that are not, and if we are really prepared to do that we may find ourselves confronted with some surprisingly radical ideas.

One of these concerns the question of national currencies. In recent centuries governments have claimed a monopoly on the issue of currency. Banks can advance credit but only the government has the right to issue money in the form of legal tender. In Europe it is now, of course, proposed that this process of centralisation should go still further: the Union itself through a central bank should issue and control the single currency that would eventually be used in all member states.

It is notable that those who favour a single currency dismiss (usually unthinkingly) the alternative proposal of a common currency. The distinction is a vital one. A single currency outlaws all others within its area of circulation; a common currency does not, it simply provides a medium of exchange that anyone is free to use (usually but not necessarily for international transactions) but it leaves national currencies still in existence for everyday purposes. The common currency can obviously be useful for businesses trading across frontiers and for travellers and holidaymakers, and if it is well managed it can provide a stable and reliable measure of value when national governments inflate their own currencies. In previous centuries gold fulfilled those functions. Pounds, Francs, Marks and all other types of money were valued against gold and the market set a figure on what they were worth. Naturally that figure fell when a dishonest or incompetent government paid its debts by printing money. Gold also worked very well as an international currency. Readers of Sterne's *Sentimental Journey* may remember how his hero sets off from London to travel around Western Europe with a pocketful of sovereigns to spend. Even until 1914 a traveller with the same coins could leave Victoria Station without a passport to visit most countries on the Continent, knowing that his sovereigns would be gladly taken wherever he went. For those who had a little gold it was easier to travel and to trade in Western Europe at the beginning of the century than it is at its end.

A common currency, then, is an excellent means of fulfilling certain clear and limited purposes, and it does so without causing a member state to lose control of an honest economic policy. The objective of a single currency in the European Union goes far beyond such a modest and sensible purpose. It is to integrate formally and irrevocably all the economies of the member states. They will be merged together into a single economy under the control of a single authority that will be (*de facto* if not *de jure*) a government; for as Keynes put it, "Whoever controls the currency controls the government." A concentration of power over 350 million people will pass into the hands of a few, and if the plan agreed in the Maastricht Treaty is put into effect the few will be the bankers, the directors of the central bank.

Britain has already experienced some of the ill-effects that followed the first step towards a single European currency. When the rates of exchange were controlled by the European Monetary System and allowed to fluctuate only within a narrow band, the result was disastrous. Britain is a major net importer in the world market and Germany a major net exporter, while Britain's direct exports to Germany are far smaller than her imports from Germany. As a result Britain's need to buy Deutschmarks was far greater than Germany's need to buy Sterling, but instead of a gradual adjustment being made by the market in the relative value of the two currencies the artificial parity was maintained until an alarming crisis blew up, the position became hopelessly unsustainable, and Britain was forced to withdraw from the ERM. Before Britain entered the ERM, Sir Alan Walters, chief economic adviser to Margaret Thatcher, predicted the disaster would happen; and although she shared his fears, their prediction was brushed aside by John Major, then Chancellor of the Exchequer, goaded on by Geoffrey Howe, Kenneth Clarke, and others in the Cabinet whose enthusiasm for monetary union outweighed their understanding of international trade.

There is nothing new about an agreement to fix exchange rates as a first step towards a single currency, as in the EMS. In 1941 almost the whole European continent was incorporated into what was called the New Economic Order. A single market far larger than what is comprised in the European Union was born after Germany's troops had invaded France in the west, Norway to the north, Rumania to the south-east, reaching Greece in the south, while Italy, Spain, and Portugal were to a greater or lesser degree in association. The then German Chancellor, Adolf Hitler, proposed to his cabinet that the Reichsmark should become the single currency for Europe. But Dr Funk, the minister for economic affairs, demurred. He argued that Germany's first objective should be to de-industrialise the rest of the Continent. Germany should become the industrial powerhouse: the rest of Europe should revert to or remain agrarian countries. They should produce the food and buy Germany's manufactured goods in exchange. This, explained Dr Funk, could best be achieved by allowing all the countries in Europe their own currencies, but with the rates of exchange being fixed in Berlin. This would let Germany sell her manufactured goods ever more favourably and become ever more rich. Not until the de-industrialisation was complete would it be in Germany's interest to make the Reichsmark into Europe's single currency. Fixed exchange rates, concluded Dr Funk, were the key, and these would be the first steps towards a single currency; but it was essential that the rates were controlled by Germany. Hitler agreed.

Since the advantages of a common currency over a single currency are so clear, one has to ask why the European Union will not recognise them. One answer lies simply in the cast of mind of those who are now settling its future. They like things to be big and unified and they distrust multiplicity. Why do all these untidy little nation states want to keep their untidy little currencies? They are bound to be a barrier against full economic and political union. Since that last aim cannot yet be publicly stated, other objections are raised, claiming that currencies, like states, must be on a large scale to be viable.

A short answer to that is that there are many countries around the world, with populations one-tenth of those of Britain or France, which have their own currencies and show no indication whatever of changing their monetary policies. Yorkshire is in population larger than Norway, Lincolnshire about the same as Iceland, and even Rutland no smaller than several independent island economies. As for the London area, there are at least thirty states with all the elements of independence, including their own currencies, which are smaller in every respect, except perhaps in geographical size. Yet this quite evidently does not damage those states economically.

In the small European countries there is little or no abject poverty to be witnessed, no beggars to accost the passer-by, no homeless huddled through the night in doorways, and no queues for a charity mug of tea, as there are in London. Nor does there tend to be a high proportion of people unemployed, as the cycle of recession and recovery is insignificant. Their economies continue at a steady pace, they seem to jog along without great ups and downs, and while only a few may become very rich, no one apparently becomes very poor.

Some economists would maintain that even within the boundaries of a nation state it is unnecessary for a government to enforce a single currency. There is in fact a tendency for this centralised power to militate against the economic well-being of the peripheral areas in which the currency circulates. The central government, being in the capital of a country, will adjoin the centres of many other activities, not least the various components of the financial industry. In a federal union this may be avoided, as Frankfurt, New York, Toronto, Sydney and Johannesburg all show, but even federal capitals will attract wealth to their midst which, in the absence of a federal government, would have remained in the regions to be spent to the advantage of people working there. Wherever the financial industry is situated, it sucks in money from outside. Investors transmit their capital to the stock exchange, the insured their premiums to the underwriters, and all who contribute to a pension fund entrust a part of their salary to the fund managers. Scarcely anyone in a modern society can escape parting with his or her money to one of those three; and, for anyone who lives in the more prosperous parts, such as Norfolk, Gloucestershire or Dorset, it will be no more spent in those counties than it will be in the case of those who sent off their cheques from Dyfed, County Durham or the furthermost corners of the Outer Hebrides. All these many billions of pounds will remain initially within the financial capital, and although most of it will further circulate out into the provinces where it can be invested most profitably in the judgement of those who have taken the money, a proportion of the many billions, having reached London, will stay there to continue circulating. As every circulation of an item of money generates at least some economic activity, it means that even if all these billions go out of London, that initial circulation of an immense sum must by itself alone transfer wealth not just from the periphery, but from all parts of the country to the financial centre.

The movement of these vast sums, which total thousands of billions of pounds in a year, also creates a major redistribution of wealth from the poorer areas to the more advantaged; and so long as investment in the private sector is necessarily directed to areas of potential growth, this cannot be avoided. One remedy is to resort to public sector investment in the areas that are being impoverished. As a policy of regional aid has been at work for many years, both at national level in the United Kingdom and France in particular and also under the auspices of the European Community, there is enough experience to judge its cost-effectiveness. Undoubtedly it has provided employment, and in the United Kingdom alone perhaps as many as a million people have had at least temporary jobs that they might not otherwise have had. Their wages will have enhanced the money circulating locally; this will also have had a beneficial effect upon the welfare of others and, as the money goes round, ever more people will be a little better off than they would have been but for the regional aid. Merseyside has received a massive amount of aid and, although it is not typical of an assisted region, it does provide a clear example of what happens. We can set aside mention of corruption and undoubted wastefulness, for there is always a danger when an exceedingly large sum of money is given away for some to go into the wrong hands, but let us instead consider the kind of scheme favoured by regional aid in most areas.

This area, the planners will say, is disadvantaged, and not until we improve the infrastructure will other investors want to come here. So new roads are to be built, and tenders invited. The main contractors chosen, their engineers and other skilled men are almost certain to come from far away, and a good proportion of their income will go back to where their homes are. They will, however, employ local sub-contractors and unskilled labour, so their money will be spent locally, although only for so long as the work lasts. The road finished, the men from far away move on and the locals go back to the job centre. Other schemes to improve the infrastructure follow, and the planners with money to spend have no trouble thinking up other forms of capital investment. In the meanwhile, investors from outside hesitate to come.

For this disappointing outcome there are two main reasons. Well-prepared schemes of public sector investment have persuaded some businesses to come into a region, but they have seldom been as many as the planners had anticipated. To some extent this has been due to a lack of confidence in the future of the economy: a board of directors with any sense of responsibility will defer plans to expand when they feel any fear of a recession, high interest rates, or uncertainties in their future markets. If theirs is an established company, already rooted elsewhere, they may feel an obligation to their present location and its people, among whom are their friends and neighbours, so they will be even less inclined to take advantage of the regional aid. There will, though, always be some businessmen tempted by the public money. That has been seen as the worst motive for a new company to set up in a region. Having been too eager to outweigh commercial considerations with the prospect of getting hold of taxpayers' money, they have often misjudged the consequences and the enterprise has collapsed. Plenty of empty premises in the assisted areas bear witness to their temptation.

The other reason for public sector investment falling far short of the benefit intended has already been touched upon. Pour a million pounds into a region and gradually, as it circulates, it will seep out of the region's economy. The larger the size of the integrated market, the quicker it will disappear, much of it into the hands of officials, administrators, legislators, pundits, brokers, financiers, social workers, and others whose interference in other people's lives inexorably grows with the size of any community. Any assisted region in a large economy cannot prevent the money given in regional aid gradually going back to where it came from, for every time it circulates some small proportion will leave the region. There are further objections to regional policies on grounds of principle: it is slow to work, it is arbitrary, and in the long-term it works against the economic well-being of the people generally who share the same currency.

In the first place, any programme of regional aid will take a long time to get underway. Not only must plans be drawn up and many discussions take place to decide how the aid is to be given and how it is to be funded, all of which may take a year or two, but the decision to give the aid can, and does, take a decade or even more. An individual town may become depressed in a matter of weeks when its local economy is founded upon a single industry that collapses at short notice. But regional policies are for whole regions, and these may take many years to fall into depression. Almost always the decline is slow to begin: individual companies find they can no longer compete; they gradually shed their labour force and invest less; once a large number of businesses share this experience, the decline in the region accelerates; unemployment then mounts as businesses go into liquidation, shops close down, mortgages are foreclosed, and bankruptcies multiply. But the crisis in hundreds of thousands of homes has to be explained to those in charge of regional policy several hundred miles away, whose remoteness keeps them blissfully unaware of the true state of the region. Members of Parliament, Mayors and Council Chairmen will then lead deputations, which troop to the centre of decision-making to lobby and plead. In the European Union, negotiations by the Commission with the national government will follow. It all takes time and it may be several years before money flows out from the centre, as the people in the blighted parts of Wales, Scotland, Cornwall and the north of England have discovered. As delay goes on, the depression deepens and more money is called for in the attempt to save the region.

Regional aid is also arbitrary; and what is arbitrary is sure to be unfair to someone. The regions must be given a boundary; a line has to be drawn. On one side the inhabitants are deemed to be in the region and eligible for assistance, while on the other side – of a road, a river, or perhaps a railway – they are to be turned away. But the people on the wrong side remain taxpayers and they must pay to assist their neighbours on the other side of the road. When businesses, especially large employers, find themselves treated arbitrarily like this, it can be the final straw to break their backs.

The aid is also arbitrary in that governments, having taken away money from the people, have to make the difficult decision: to whom are they to offer, and to whom are they to refuse, the money collected? As ordinary governments do not deal in pennies, or even thousands of pounds, but millions, so the superstate decides with hundreds of millions. These are sums of money that great mega-corporations understand, but are far beyond the ken of the average businessman who forms the backbone of a healthy economy. As noted in another chapter, it is not for nothing that all the great transnational companies have their lobbying posts maintained within striking distance of the offices of both the national governments of the larger member states and the Commission in Brussels. As their purpose is to keep in touch with the decision-makers, it is not very difficult for them to submit their cases for aid to those whom they already know and who have a grasp of their affairs. To compete against highly-paid and experienced lobbyists is a tall order for the smaller company – the kind, say that employs two or three hundred – and, in pursuit of official aid, the truly small businessman is completely out of his depth. Even if the officials discount the skilful special pleading and make every effort to be fair, not even Solomon in his wisest mood would be able to allocate those hundreds of millions of pounds with objective justice.

The fourth objection is that if regional aid continues as it must do to succeed, it will do long-term damage to the whole economy in which the single currency circulates. As a regional policy increases expenditure, extra revenue has to be raised (unless inflation is resorted to) and the higher taxation must necessarily come from the whole corpus of taxpayers. A net gain by those in the assisted regions is matched by a net loss by everyone outside. As a means of redistributing wealth from rich to poor it may seem fair, but that is not quite what happens. Because taxation in the European Union is mainly indirect, notably in the forms of VAT and import levies, the burden falls proportionally more heavily on those with lower incomes than those in higher brackets. Thus the comparatively poor will pay *per capita* a higher proportion of the cost of the aid, while in the regions a large slice of the cake will go to the more powerful (usually the richer) rather than their competitors. This diversion of wealth has a further effect. Profitable industries are forced by taxation to subsidise unprofitable ones, yet a company's profitability is a measure of how much the consumer is willing to spend on its products while a decline in profitability is, as a rule, an indication of how much its products have fallen out of favour. To tax a profitable business is necessary and just, but there comes a point when a higher rate of taxation will prevent it from serving the public as the latter would wish. A regional policy carried on over a long period will, therefore, drain wealth away from where the consuming public has chosen it to be and transfer it elsewhere. With any long-term policy of regional aid, the sum of economic well-being diminishes, and goes on diminishing at an increasing rate.

These objectives can be minimised by regional policy being left in the hands of nation-states. The smaller the self-governing state, the less the objections will arise, as the need for regional policies decreases with the scale of the economy. This leads to the only way to overcome all the objections that have been discussed. When a nation-state allows its currency to float freely, it acquires an import control that acts naturally, immediately, without being arbitrary, without any one interest group exerting its influence to the detriment of others, and without unfairly damaging the economy as a whole, or treating consumers, especially the less well-off, with any degree of unfairness. However, a floating currency puts power in the hands of the people instead of government, and in Brussels that is a grievous fault.

If we can agree that nation states should not be deprived of control over their own currencies, could we go further? As the regions in the European Union are themselves the size of small states, can we not devise a currency system that will give the regions the same advantages that the small states enjoy? A number of independent economists have urged a multi-level system: a common currency for international trade, national currencies and, for the larger countries, local or regional currencies. Both David Weston and James Robertson have written about this proposal in the journal *New European*: and the latter's excellent book *Future Wealth* has set out the groundwork for a multi-level currency system, along with other far-reaching policies to avert the collapse of Western economies, which he foresees beginning before the end of the century. The simplest step towards local currencies would be to give permission to local government authorities to share the national government's monopoly.

David Weston has told how, during the 1930's, the Burgomaster of Worgl in Austria issued tickets for 'services rendered' which were treated as money within the area. Authorising various schemes of public works, he gave employment to many who would otherwise have been idle, and paid them with these tickets. Being backed by the local authority, they were accepted by shopkeepers and others. As a measure of their success it was calculated that each ticket circulated some twenty times. Apart from the employment promoted by the scheme, the extra economic activity generated by the circulation of these tickets brought much more prosperity to Worgl than the sensible burgomaster had foreseen. No less than two hundred other burgomasters announced that they would follow his lead, but the prospect of an alternative currency throughout much of Austria posed a threat to the National Bank. It asked the Supreme Court to uphold its monopoly, the judges agreed to do so, and the scheme came to an end.

In the case of Britain, all that would be necessary would be for Parliament to give the go-ahead by removing some of the constraints that have been imposed upon local government authorities. There is a danger that the Commission of the European Union might claim that the devolution was against the spirit, if not the letter, of the Treaty of Maastricht. A complaint could then be referred to the European Court of Justice, but the outcome would probably depend upon how resolute the British Government was willing to be. Such difficulties over, the local government could then issue a currency in the form of IOU's. The local banks might demur at the additional work, but there seems no practical reason why these IOU's should not evolve into a local currency. Employers, both the local public bodies and businesses in the area, could offer all or part of their wages in the local currency at a slight premium to encourage employees to take up the offer, and local taxes could be paid in the same system at a slight discount. If the premium/discount system attracted local businessmen as a means of buying and selling in their own area, the new currency would stimulate the local economy and, as the notes went round, the prosperity of the area would increase.

Once liberated to do so, local authorities could devise their own model of what they wanted. If the local banks saw the likelihood of the area prospering, it would be in their interests to support the scheme, and it would not be beyond their wit to introduce two parallel systems of accounts. Western Europe, like the United States, is poised to see a revolution in how we buy and sell. Electronic debiting and crediting is on the way. Cash in our pockets will be almost unnecessary, as bits of plastic take its place. Even cheques will be of a declining use in our lives. Business transactions of every kind, no matter how large, will be carried out with electronic aids. Although currency in the form of notes and coins will have only a minor part in the economic life of a modern society, its denotations will remain as the benchmark of any other currency. That need be no bar to a multiplicity of currencies in any nation-state. How many? That is a question not for economists or bankers to answer, but the people themselves through their elected representatives. In a word, currencies will be democratised.

Clearly any proposal of this sort runs counter to the whole philosophy of the European Union as it now is. So far from multiplying currencies the federalists want to outlaw all but one, the Euro. This is just one example of their rigidity and their imperviousness to any suggestion that we should encourage diversity rather than uniformity. If the arguments in this book have any validity the course they want to take us on is a very dangerous one, and before we are irrevocably committed to it we should pause and think seriously about what we are doing. What sort of Europe do we really want to live in? What changes must we make if we are going to get it?

The root of it all is that the European Union must change some of its most cherished presuppositions. It must do more than pay lip-service to some vaguely defined principle of subsidiarity and recognise that a small political unit is, as such, likely to be more humane and more efficient than a large one. We should only interfere in its workings if there is a clearly proved benefit to be gained, and furthermore that benefit must be to the good of the people as a whole, not to the politicians, the bureaucrats, or the large corporations. On balance, more power now needs to be returned to the member states than is taken away from them.

The acid test of whether a problem needs a European solution rather than a national one is quite simply whether it crosses frontiers. Huge numbers of things that the Union now considers its province would be ruled out by that test. They are done in the name of uniformity and would certainly be returned to the member states or the regions if we recognised what is true in politics as it is in ecology. Variety means health. Uniformity when it is imposed artificially means that something is going wrong.

The most obvious example of a problem that crosses frontiers is the environment. No one country can solve the problems of pollution and degradation if the countries around it persist in destructive habits. The natural world does not recognise man-made political demarcations. Yet if we look at the major environmental problems facing us it is clear that even the European Union is too small to solve them. This is plainly true of the great world-wide crises, the destruction of the ozone layer, global warming, the felling of the rain forests, the extinction of species, the over-fishing of the seas, and so on. It is also true of what looks like local problems, such as the impending biological death of the North Sea. The rivers of twelve countries disgorge their filth and poison into it but only six of them are in the European Union; the other six are outside. Much the same can be said of the Mediterranean. A Europe capable of solving that urgent problem would have to include the countries of Eastern Europe. That is yet another reason why we should bring them in, but if we are to so we must abandon any idea that the European Union can continue down its present road towards becoming a super-state. It is not just that Eastern Europeans have had too much trouble regaining their national independence to part with it to Brussels, nor that the Union's institutions would have to cope with even more varying demands (the European Parliament, with some forty languages in full spate might resemble feeding time at the zoo as much as the Tower of Babel). The practical problems would be overwhelming unless we were prepared to show a flexibility that at present is wholly lacking. The Common Agricultural Policy, extended to the East, would create such vast surpluses of grain and dairy products that the Union would soon be bankrupt or the farmers of Western Europe reduced to penury. Unemployment in the West would worsen as companies transferred their factories to the East to take advantage of wage costs a fraction of what they are in the West.

It would, nevertheless, be perfectly possible to accommodate the enlargement of the European Union to take in the whole of Europe provided we were ready to make the necessary adjustments to the structure of the Union. If those adjustments were damaging we would need to ask whether it was worth it, but the fact is that most of them would be greatly to our benefit in any case. If we take the Common Agricultural Policy as an example, how many European families would grieve if they were told that in future they would save £1,000 a year on food prices while farming became more environmentally friendly and good farmers were no worse off? The only shame is that, without some crisis to kick us into action we seem set to tolerate the extravagance and abuses of the Common Agricultural Policy into the indefinite future.

The same applies to the constitution of the European Union as a customs union rather than a free trade area. Eastern European countries are now on the wrong end of this policy which inevitably discriminates against countries outside the Union: that, after all, is the point. If they come into the Union they would not want to have their own patterns of trade disrupted by the European Union system of tariffs and restrictions; but then we would all benefit by dismantling it and allowing member states to set their own rules within the limits laid down by an agreement to replace the customs union with a free trade area. The difference between the two is important: as noted already, a free trade area brings down the barriers between member states while leaving them free to trade as they wish with outside countries, while in a customs union that freedom is surrendered.

And as to the abandonment of the 'European dream', the creation of a single mega-state, we should all be better off for that, even the ordinary people of France and Germany. Their rulers, though, would have to recognise that the Franco-German coalition, which has up to now been the axis of the Union, would be overwhelmed by other alliances in the new, complete Europe.

In short, the creation of a true European Union, embracing the whole continent, would force us to do what we should already be doing in our own interest, conducting an audit of all the Union structures and regulations, those that exist and those that are planned, and deciding which are beneficial and which are not.

On the positive side we could start by looking at three organisations that have an impressive record of achievement, much of it unknown to the public. They are the Council of Europe (not to be confused with the Council of Ministers), the Economic Commission for Europe, and the Conference on Security and Co-operation in Europe. To do justice to these institutions would take many pages, but a summary will show that they each have an immense potential for further development.

Membership of these bodies is not restricted to countries in the European Union. Thirty-six countries are in the Council of Europe, thirty-five in the Economic Commission for Europe, and fifty-two in the Conference on Security and Co-operation in Europe. The two latter include Canada and the United States, the anomaly being explained by the role they play in the United Nations and NATO.

The work of all three is done internationally, or inter-governmentally, and consequently with every principle of democracy. They recognise that there is a diversity of national interests in Europe and none of them make any attempt to coerce any one of the nations to agree to any measure that is contrary to its interests. No rows, outbursts of indignation, no ministers storming out in anger, no talk of vetoes, or rumours of horse-trading ever emanates from their meetings. For the media, therefore, they make boring copy, which is why most people know little or nothing about them, but because they quietly reach agreement and are seldom too ambitious they have been remarkably successful. Together they could serve all the purposes of the European peoples when their problems cross the frontiers.

For the Council of Europe the test for membership requires every member country to accept the rule of law and to ensure that its people enjoy certain fundamental freedoms. Its Parliamentary Assembly meets at Strasbourg in a building also lent to the European Union's Parliament, and each member country sends a delegation drawn from its own national parliament. The Assembly has plenary sessions, but its principal work is undertaken by thirteen specialist committees, which cover most governmental functions that can cross frontiers, except for defence and foreign affairs. These committees are solely deliberative: having examined an issue, they make recommendations to the Committee of Ministers, which is the Council's executive organ and, as its name suggests, consists of ministers from each member country desiring to take part. The Committee may pass a resolution or agree to a convention. A resolution sets out the measures that it believes a member country should take to put into effect a common policy. A convention is an agreement that binds the member countries whose ministers have signed it. A well-known example of the latter is the European Convention on Human Rights, which interprets and specifies certain fundamental freedoms. Not every member country has signed it, but those that have agreed to introduce laws giving effect to the Convention. This illustrates two of the Council's working principles. No country is coerced by majority voting, for there is no compulsion to take part in formulating a resolution or convention, and a country only joins in when its representatives believe it is in its interests to do so. Nor is there any attempt to usurp the power of the national parliaments, for any change in the law must be made by them.

The Economic Commission for Europe, an agency of the United Nations, was set up to raise 'the level of European economic activity', and to maintain and strengthen 'the economic relations of the European countries'. That was in 1947. Just a decade later it extended its scope to include environmental issues, being the first international body to do so. Committees exist to consider the problems of each of Europe's main industries; like the Council of Europe's Committee of Ministers it can pass a resolution about action that should be taken by member countries, and in each case it strives to avoid opt-outs, although in practice this is seldom necessary. The reason is that the Committee will only take up an issue if it believes there is a general agreement among the governments to achieve some co-ordinated action. Who better to decide this than the Committee members who are representing the governments? Many of the resolutions may be about mundane matters, yet notable achievements have been made. Once every country in Europe had its own laws to regulate inland transport, traffic signs and standards of driving; now they are almost the same throughout the Continent, the changes having come without any country feeling imposed upon or aggrieved by the Economic Commission for Europe, the author of the changes. This Commission's role is different from its counterpart in the European Union; it is the servant not the master of the member countries.

Then there is the Conference on Security and Co-operation in Europe. The Helsinki Final Act of 1975 is intended to be a politically, not legally, binding agreement that has three main sections. The first concerns security between the participating states and is really a declaration as to how one state should behave towards another. The second section extends to co-operation in the field of economics, of science and technology, and the environment. The third section is about the protection of human rights. The Conference may be said to be in a state of adolescence, its infancy over. With the fall of the Iron Curtain and a membership of no less than fifty-two, it is there to be used, given the will to do so.

These three have one defect, and in the eyes of the leaders of the political class it is a most grievous defect. Power stays with the peoples of Europe. The two weapons of government (legislation and taxation) are not lifted from where they should belong to be concentrated into the hands of a few. It is a disappointment too for the heads of the great transnational corporations who naturally prefer to deal with one mega-state than with a multiplicity of small governments. Like the heads of the political class, they revel in the concentration of power, but the *modus operandi* of each of these three bodies avoids the concentration of power they relish. The very fact that the identities of the states remain separate ensures a further distribution of decision-making. Far from offending against any principle of democracy, every step any one of these three may take has to be taken with the approval of the elected representatives of the people, for the latter retain control over the two acts of coercion (legislation and taxation) that have been referred to so often in this book, and on which any government is dependent to put any policy into effect.

If these three are capable of promoting and co-ordinating the cross-frontier co-operation of Europe's peoples, why do we need the European Union, limited as it is to only a part of Europe? Logic suggests it is unnecessary. If it is to be kept then it must be radically reformed, for in its present form it is, to put it bluntly, obsolete. The whole concept belongs to an earlier period in history, before the coming of the global market and the information revolution made political boundaries largely irrelevant to economic activity. We are in a world of economic interdependence. Brussels can issue as many directives and regulations as it likes, but it cannot stop money being moved about electronically in vast amounts. The World Trade Organisation is also a fact of life: it has the supranational power to facilitate trade in goods and services, and its role in the world is not unlike that of the European Economic Community in the original Common Market. In the context of trade the European Union has become not just superfluous but positively harmful, for individual states need to retain some control over the effects of inter-state trade in case parts of their economies need temporary protection, the most effective form of protection being a separate currency.

The attempt to override national interests has already produced considerable friction, for example in the imposition of the Common Fisheries Policy on Britain, which finds itself in a minority of one with its legitimate interests steam-rollered. That sort of disharmony is bound to proliferate as more and more uniformity is imposed. The only solution is to abandon the whole principle of supranationality. It must be replaced by an intergovernmental approach in which each state retains the right to participate in an European policy, but equally the right not to do so. There could still be a role for the Commission, not as the exclusive proposer of legislation but as a secretariat to serve the inter-governmental conferences where common policies would be forged, to be ratified afterwards by each state according to its own legislative procedure. Each common policy would then be enshrined in a treaty and be subject to international law. In this more modest role, the Commission could fill in the gaps left by the other three European bodies. But in a Europe where the interests of the people come first, there would be more work done by those three bodies and so no gaps to fill.

The present European Union is both too small and too large. It is too small not just because it includes only a minority of European countries but also because, in the economic sphere, it faces world-wide commercial

91

and technological forces that it can never hope to control. It is too large because, for all the reasons with which this book has been concerned, people are happier, more fulfilled, and better governed when the unit of government is scaled down. It must be small enough for all the people in one state to know that, whatever differences of opinion there may be between them they are all members of a coherent society to which they feel a common sense of belonging. Such a state may need to be smaller than the largest states in Europe today: quite certainly it needs to be very much smaller than a centralised European Union.

When Leopold Kohr put the case for the small state in his *Breakdown of Nations* he added a chapter entitled 'But will it be done?' It must be one of the shortest chapters of any book ever written: "No!" His ideal was that the human race should divide itself into self-governing entities all of roughly the same modest size and co-operating in such a way that none can threaten or dominate another. As we move into the electronic age something akin to his ideal will become attainable. The marvels of this new ages will empower the people. They will break down Europe.

References

Adler (1928). *Understanding Human Nature,* transl. Beranworlf, Walter: Allen and Unwin.

Body, Richard (1990). *Europe of Many Circles*: New European Publications.

Creighton, Mandell (1882-1894). *History of the Papacy*: Longmans. Green.

Dixon, Norman (1976). *Psychology of Military Incompetence*: Cape.

Gates, Bill (1995). *The Road Ahead*: Viking.

Hayek, F. A. (1944). *The Road to Serfdom*: Routledge.

Kohr, Leopold (1957). *The Breakdown of Nations*: Routledge and Kegan Paul.

Robertson, James (1989). *Future Wealth*: Cassell.

Selborne, David (1994). *Principle of Duty*: Sinclair. Stevenson.

Sterne, Lawrence (1900). *Sentimental Journey*: Dent: Everyman Library.

Index

accountability 54
acid rain 5
Acton, Lord 8-10
Adenaeur, Konrad 33
Adler 41
advertising 16
alienation 3, 37
America (see also; United States; constitution) revolution 33, 74
Andalusia 58
Andorra 13, 15
Arab world 11
architecture 47-49
Aristotle 34, 47, 71
arts, the 46
Asia 18, 19, 58, 62
Athens, classical 45-6
Australia 11, 72
Austria, 28, 48, 85
authority 9
autocracy 10, 11
autonomy 75
averages, human, 45

Bach, Johann Sebastian 47
Bacon, Francis 8
Balfour, Arthur 41
banks 19
barriers to trade 21
Basques 60, 68
Bavaria 60, 66, 68, 72
Beethoven 47
Belgium 22
Bentham, Jeremy 33
Berlaymont 64
Berlin 49, 59
Berne 75

Big Government 64
bigness 5, 10, 25
Birmingham 18, 67
Bismark, Count Otto von 47
Bonn 59
Bossi, Umberto 59
Breakdown of Nations, The 7, 92
Bretons 60, 66, 68
Britain *see also* United Kingdom 21, 23, 31, 36, 43, 51, 53, 56, 60-61, 73, 76, 78-79, 85, 91
British Empire 24, 27
Brussels 4, 6, 22, 28, 39, 41, 53, 57, 62, 64, 73, 76, 83, 87
Bulgaria 58
bureaucracy 3-4, 56
Burke, Edmund 11

Caligula 11
Canada 29, 72
canton 75
CAP 36, 53, 56, 87
capitalism 26
Castro, Fidel 11
Catalans 58, 60
Central African Federation 72
centralisation of Europe 4, 13, 21-22, 24, 56
Charlemagne 11, 51
Chechnya 2, 29
Chicago 11, 27
China 2, 17, 18, 42
Church of England 36
citizens 37, 52
citizenship 3, 4, 54, 60, 62
civil, civic bond 35, 37, 51
civil servants 8, 9, 38, 42, 46, 52

Clarke, Kenneth 79
Coca Cola 12
colonies 13, 26, 29
Commission, European 22, 53, 70, 76, 82, 83, 85, 91
Commissioners, European 41
Committee of Ministers (Council of Europe) 89
Committee of the Regions 60, 76
Common Agricultural Policy; *see* CAP
Common Currency 77-78
Common Fisheries Policy 56, 91
Common Market 62, 91
commune 75-76
communism *see also* Marxism 27, 43
community 32, 34-5, 48, 51, 57, 62
competition 21
confederal 75
Congress of Vienna 75
consumption of goods 16
constituency 54
constituents 41
constitution, American 34
Cornwall 82
corporations 8, 21, 22
corruption 9, 81
Corsica 68
Côte d'Azur 67
Council of Europe 71, 88-90
Council of Ministers 52, 53-54, 61, 70, 72
County Durham 80
Court of Auditors 36
Creighton, Bishop Mantell 8
crime 3, 31-2, 36, 51
CSCE (Conference on Security and Co-operation in Europe) 88, 90
Cuba 11
currency *see also* single currency 13, 19, 77, 79-80, 84, 86
currency, local 84-85
customs unions 20, 87-88

Cyprus 25
Czech Republic 58

Declaration of Independence 74
Delors, Jacques 76
democracies 11
democracy 5, 7, 37, 38-40, 52, 54, 58, 69, 75
democratic deficit 52, 53, 61
Denmark 27
dependencies 13
Deutschmarks 59, 78
devolution 8, 35
Devonshire 67
Dickens, Charles 67
dictatorships 11, 68
diplomats 52
directives 53, 57
dirigiste 19
disintegration (of EU) 4
dissidents 68
Dixon, Norman 9
Dorset 80
Duever 47
dumping 20
Dusseldorf 67
Dutch *see* Holland
Dyfed 80

East, the 18, 19, 58
Eastern Europe 21, 58, 87-88
Economic Commission for Europe 88, 89-90
economic cycle 80
economic union 79
economists 15
economy, local 17
  global 17
  Marxist vs. capitalist 26
  of scale 57
  Western 84
elections 40
electors 37
Elgar, Edward 47

Elizabethan age 45
electronic voting 69
elite 69-70
e-mail 63
empowerment 68
EMU *see* single currency
EMS 79
England *see also* Church 12, 47, 49,
    54, 58
  revolution 33
  system of government 11
English language 66
  literature 45
enlargement 87
environment 5
ERM *see* Exchange Rate Mechanism
Estonia 29
Euro *see* single currency
Eurocrats 6
Europe *see also* Western Europe 1,
    4, 6, 10-12, 17-18, 22, 26, 31,
    36, 47-49, 51, 52, 55-57, 60-62,
    66, 69-70, 72, 74, 76-77, 80, 88,
    90-92
European Commission *see*
  Commission
European Convention on Human
  Rights 89
European Court of Justice 52, 85
'European dream' 88
European Economic Community 11,
    33, 52-53, 59, 68, 74, 75, 81, 91
Europeanisation 57, 59, 66-67
European Parliament *see* parliament
Europeans 36, 42
Europe of Many Circles 5
European Union 1-2, 4-6, 12, 17-
    18, 20-21, 23, 25, 28, 32, 36, 38-
    39, 42, 51, 55-61, 66, 72-74, 76-
    79, 82, 86-88, 90, 91-92
Eurosceptic 52
ever-closer union 63
exchange rates 79
Exchange Rate Mechanism 78-79

Falangists 27
family 34
Farber, M.L. 9
fascism 27
fashion, rule by 16
federalism 1, 51, 55
  federalists 25, 26, 52, 59, 70, 86
  Federal Letter of Switzerland 74
  federal union 4, 6, 17, 20, 24, 72,
    73, 74, 80
federation 22, 25, 28
feudalism 8, 32-3
Finland 66
fishing, over- 5, 87
Flemings 58
flight of wealth 19
Foreign Office 40
Franc, French 78
France 19, 21, 28, 31, 56, 57-58,
    76, 79, 81, 88
  French Revolution 33
Franco, General 27
Franco-German wars 2, 25
Frankfurt 18, 80
fraud 36
freedom 7
free trade 2, 18, 19, 20, 88
Friends of the Earth 37
fundamentalists 35, 41
Funk, Dr. 79
Future Wealth 84

Galileo 45
Gates, Bill 68-69
GATT 21, 53, 63
General Motors 18, 21
Germany 21, 26, 27, 28, 31, 33,
    47-48, 57-59, 72, 74, 76-79, 88
  economic miracle 24
  unification 28, 56
Gilbert and Sullivan 47
Glasgow 67
global alliances 64
Global Paradox 3, 12, 63-64

globalisation 12, 55, 63
global warming 5
Gloucestershire 80
Goldsmith, Sir James 19
Gold Standard 78
government 39, 40
  British form of 43
governments 11, 41
  international vs. supranational 71
Great Britain *see* Britain
Greece 25, 43, 79
  ancient 47

Haiti 10
Hapsburgs 74
harmonisation 12
Hayek, Professor F.A. 40
Heath, Edward 76
Helsinki Final Act (1975) 90
Herine 47
History of the Papacy 8
Hitler, Adolf 11, 27, 41, 51, 79
Holbein, Hans 47
Holland, system of government 11
homogeneity 42-43, 49, 72
horse trading 54
House of Commons *see also*
  Parliament 36, 53-54
Howe, Geoffrey 79
Hungary 58

Iceland 21, 23, 31, 36, 79
imperialism 27
independence 4, 13, 29, 35, 77
India 18, 27, 39
individual, the 63-64
Indonesia 18, 39
industries 16
  British 20, 24
inefficiency of European Union 56
inevitability 61
information technology 3
inner cities 67
integration 12, 22

interest rates 19
intergovernmental co-operation 5
inter-war years 25
investment 19
Iran 35
Ireland 65-66
Iron Curtain 90
Italy 31, 33, 49, 58-59, 76, 79
Ivan the Terrible 8, 11
Japan 23-24
jingoists 4, 6
Johannesburg 11, 80
Johnson, Ben 47
*Journal of Abnormal Social
  Psychology* 9
journalists 40
Julius Caesar 51
justice 71

Kant, Emmanuel 47
Keynes, John Maynard 78
Kiev 59
Kissinger, Henry 8
Kohl, Helmut 76
Kohr, Leopold 7-8, 92
Korea 13

labour 15
länder 48, 59, 72
Latvia 29
law 36
leader, party 37
Left, the 34
legal profession 33
Lenin 7, 68
liberals 8, 33
Lincolnshire 79
Liechtenstein 7, 21, 23, 77
Lithuania 29
Liverpool 67
Locke, John 33
Lombardy 59
London 31, 38, 46-49, 60, 79, 80
Luton 67

Lyons 18

Madrid 49
Major, John 79
Malaysia 18, 23
Manchester 67
manifestos 39, 55
Mao Tse Tung 11, 42
markets 15, 17, 20
  mass-marketing 16
Marlowe, Christopher 47
Marx, Karl 26
Marxism 26
materialism 34
media 36, 37, 40-41, 53
Mediterranean 87
medium-sized businesses 22
mega-businessmen 51
megastate 3-4, 41-43
Members, of Parliament *see* MPs,
  of the European Parliament
  see MEPs
mercantile class 33
MEPs 54-55
Merseyside 81
Mexico 29
Microsoft 68
migration 48-9, 66
Milan 18
Mill, John Stuart 6, 33
minorities 5, 38-39, 41
Mississippi 27
modus vivendi 21
monetary policies 19
Monnet, Jean 33, 63, 66
monopoly 17
moral, consensus 35
  health 35
  questions 36
Moscow 4, 58
Montesquieu, Simon de 75
Mozart 47
MPs 38, 54, 82
multinational 2, 22

Munich 60

NAFTA 29
Naisbitt, John 3, 12, 56, 63-64
Napoleon, Bonaparte 11, 27, 51,
  74-75
  Napoleonic wars 28
nation 1, 9, 13, 20
national debt 19
nationalism 55
nation state 1, 2, 5-6, 13, 21, 25,
  28, 29, 51, 52, 56, 77, 83-84, 86
NATO 29, 71
Nazis 55
neo-Nazis, 59
Netherlands *see* Holland
networking 64-65
New Economic Order 11, 79
New European 84
Newton 45
New York 46, 80
New Zealand 3, 23, 38-39, 57
Nietzsche, Friedrich 47
Nigeria 2
Norfolk 80
Norman epoch 32
North of England 83
Northern Ireland 25, 59
North Sea 87
Norway 2, 3, 23, 27, 31, 36, 39, 79

Olympics 13
Oslo 39
Oprichniki 8
Oprichnina 8
Outer Hebrides 80
overregulatio, 56
ozone layer 87

Pacific Union, putative 23
Papa Doc Duvalier 10
Paris 46, 49, 59
Parliament *see also* House of
  Commons 6, 9, 36, 40, 54

European 52, 54, 70, 87, 89
Russian 8
Parliamentary Assembly (Council of
Europe) 89
party, machine 39
political 39, 46
patriotism 55
pension funds 19
Persian Empire 45
Perth 72
Philadelphia 75
Pittsburgh 18
plastic cards 86
Plato 47
Poland 58
police 32
politicians 8, 40, 42, 51
psychology of 9-10
pollution 86-87
population 7
Portugal 27, 66, 79
Empire 27
Pound Sterling 78
poverty 31
power, pursuit of 8, 12
corruption by 9, 12, 52
pressure groups 37-39, 46
princes 48
Principle of Duty 34-35
product 17
propaganda 4, 60
prosperity 15-16
protectionism 2, 17, 26
protectorates 13
Provence 66
Prussia 47, 72
Psychology of Military Incompetence
9
punishment 32, 36

Quebec 72

racism 55
rain forests 5, 87

raw materials 26
recession 16-17
'Reference man' 42
referendum 4, 60
of California 77
of Norway 23
regional aid 58, 81-84
'states' 76
regulations 6
Reichsmark 79
Renaissance 45, 49
revolution 33, 68
Rhode Island 73
Right, the 34
rights 34, 37
Road Ahead, The 69
Road to Serfdom, The 40
Road Haulage Federation 37
Robertson, James 84
Robespierre 68
Roman Empire 11, 27, 47
Romansch 74
Rome 46
Roosevelt, Franklin Delanore 73
Rumania 79
Russia 8, 11, 25, 28, 33, 43, 58
Rutland 79
Rwanda 27

Schopenhauer 47
Schuman, Rober, 33, 63, 66
Scotland 35, 57, 59, 66, 82
Second World War 25, 29, 33, 77
Selbourne, David 34-35
self-confidence, national 24
Sentimental Journey 78
Shakespeare 47
shipbuilding, British 17
Sicily 59
silent majority 38-39
Singapore 18
Single Currency 4, 60, 77-80, 83,
86
Single European Act 72

Single Market 17, 22
Sixth Fleet 27
Slough 67
Slovakia 58
small businesses 16-17
small states 46
socialism 34
socialists 26
social security 2
social services 19
society 7, 8, 31, 36, 55, 71
sovereignty 5-6, 29, 60, 71-72
Soviet Bloc 34
Soviet Union *see* USSR
Spaak 33
Spain 27, 59, 76, 79
speeches 55
spin doctors 55
Spinelli, Altiero 63, 66
Sterne 78
St. Petersburg 59
Stalin 11
standardisation 90
state, as an entity 11
    optimum size of 3, 7-8, 10
Strasbourg 54
subsidiarity 60
subsidies 57
superhighway 63
superpowers 13, 28
superstate 12, 18, 28, 61, 83
supranationalism 6, 18, 20, 56, 71-72
Sweden 23, 27, 39, 43
Switzerland 2, 3, 21, 23, 57, 73-77
Sydney 72, 80

tabloids 39
Taparelli d'Azeglio, Miasma 59
taxation 5, 52, 58, 83-84, 90
technology of the future 63-65, 67
telecommunications 63, 68
telecomputer 65, 68, 69
television 37, 39, 40

Texas 73
Thatcher, Margaret 78-79
Tonga 23
Toronto 80
totalitarianism 19
Tower of Babel 65, 87
Toytown 10
trade associations 37
trade union, 24, 46
transnationals 23
treaty, power to make 5
    of Maastricht 23, 52, 53, 60, 72, 73, 76, 78, 85
    of Rome 23, 33, 52, 72
Turkey 25
Tuscany 66-67
Tyneside 67

Ukraine 58
unemployment 19, 57, 80
unification, of Europe 13
uniformity 12, 22
Understanding Human Nature 41
UNFAO 42
United Kingdom *see also* Britain 12, 76, 81
United Nations 12, 13, 71, 77, 89
United States of America 2, 3, 17, 18, 19, 23, 28, 29, 31, 72-75, 77, 85
    civil war 72
    constitution 73
    presidential elections 37
    Supreme Court 73
urban decline and renewal 67
USSR 25, 28, 29, 72

vandalism 32
VAT 52, 83-84
Victorian epoch 20, 45, 47
Vietnam 13, 19
vigilantism 32
Voltaire 33
voter, power of 37

Wales 35, 59-60, 68, 82
Wall Street Journal 74
Walloons 57, 68
Walters, Sir Alan 78
wars, chance of 20
Warsaw 59
Washington D.C. 38, 73, 75
wealth 17
West, the 18, 19, 32, 34, 39, 58
  decline of 61
Western Europe 3, 13, 23, 25, 31,
  33, 36, 39, 61, 75, 78, 85, 87

West Indian Federation 72
Weston, David 84-85
Whitehall 75
Worgl, 85
World Review 12
World Trade Organisation 21, 53,
  91

Yorkshire 79
Yugoslavia 2, 25, 27, 72

Zurich 75